macromedia

flash™ to the core

an interactive sketchbook

by joshua davis

Flash to the Core:
An Interactive Sketchbook by Joshua Davis

International Standard Book Number: 0-7357-1288-3

Library of Congress Catalog Card Number: 00-111651

Printed in the United States of America

First Printing: August 2002

06 05 04 03 02   7 6 5 4 3 2 1

Interpretation of the printing code: The rightmost double-digit number is the year of the book's printing; the rightmost single-digit number is the number of the book's printing. For example, the printing code 02-1 shows that the first printing of the book occurred in 2002.

Trademarks

Warning and Disclaimer

Publisher
David Dwyer

Associate Publisher
Stephanie Wall

Executive Editor
Steve Weiss

Production Manager
Gina Kanouse

Managing Editor
Sarah Kearns

Acquisitions Editor
Theresa Gheen

Development Editor
Linda Laflamme

Project Editor
Jake McFarland

Copy Editor
Chrissy Andry

Product Marketing Manager
Kathy Malmloff

Publicity Manager
Susan Nixon

Manufacturing Coordinator
Jim Conway

Cover Designers
Joshua Davis
Jemma Gura (www.prate.com)

Interior Designers
Joshua Davis
Wil Cruz

Chapter Break Designers
Joshua Davis
Mike Cina (www.trueistrue.com)

Compositor
Wil Cruz

Proofreader
Benjamin Lawson

Indexer
Lisa Stumpf

Table of Contents

ABOUT THE AUTHOR

 Joshua Davis is an artist and technologist producing both public and private work on and off the web. His site, **www.praystation.com**, was the winner of the 2001 Prix Ars Electronica Golden Nica in the category of Net Excellence, the highest honor in international Net art and design. Award-winning commercial endeavors include **www.barneys.com** and **www.motown.com**, to name a few. He attended Pratt Institute in Brooklyn, majoring in Communication Design and Illustration, with a minor in Art History. Joshua is an instructor at the School of Visual Arts in New York City, and he lectures globally on his work, inspirations, and motivations. He lives with his wife, Melissa, in Port Washington, New York.

Studio/Business Inquiries:

Joshua Davis/Praystation
130 Shore Road, #202
Port Washington, New York 11050

Studio Fax: 1.516.883.5505

flashtothecore@praystation.com

About the Tech Editors

Todd Marks, formerly a high school math teacher, has been filling in the left-brained activity at digitalorganism since 2000. Todd has worked extensively with Flash ActionScript, PHP, Lingo, and many other development languages, placing cutting-edge code in several projects, including digitalorganism's award-winning site. Todd is also a Macromedia Certified Subject Matter Expert.

Geoff Stearns is a designer, Flash developer, and contributor to *Macromedia Flash: Super Samurai*. Based in Tucson, AZ, Geoff spends too much time on the Internet and keeps a record of his time wasted at **www.deconcept.com**.

Acknowledgments

I would like to thank the very patient and amazing team at New Riders: Steve Weiss, David Dwyer, Theresa "The Whip" Gheen, Linda Laflamme, Jake McFarland, Sarah Kearns, Susan Nixon, Wil "The Man" Cruz, and everyone else, who have given me this platform to voice my ideas and to help educate the next generation of artists and designers.

I would also like to thank Mia Amato, who somehow managed to put up with my ever-changing personalities over the course of the year while we wrote this book.

Never-ending thanks to my peers and friends who provided valuable assistance both directly and indirectly by allowing me to poke and prod into their psyches: Branden Hall, Erik Natzke, Robert Hodgin, Colin Moock, Geoff Stearns, Jeremy Clark, Eric "eman" Wittman, Jared Tarbell, Yugo Nakamura, Manny Tan, Matt Owens, Lee MisenHeimer, Eddie Pak, SK Lam, the old Kioken crew, Michael Cina, Jemma Gura, Mike Young, and shapeshifter.

And heartfelt thanks to my wife, Melissa, and our families. Thank you for your love, support, and motivation.

—Joshua Davis

A Message from New Riders

As the reader of this book, you are our most important critic and commentator. We value your opinion and want to know what we're doing right, what we could do better, in what areas you'd like to see us publish, and any other words of wisdom you're willing to pass our way.

As Executive Editor at New Riders, I welcome your comments. You can fax, email, or write me directly to let me know what you did or didn't like about this book—as well as what we can do to make our books better. When you write, please be sure to include this book's title, ISBN, and author, as well as your name and phone or fax number. I will carefully review your comments and share them with the authors and editors who worked on the book.

Please note that I cannot help you with technical problems related to the topic of this book, and that due to the high volume of email I receive, I might not be able to reply to every message. Thanks.

Fax   317-581-4663

Email: **steve.weiss@newriders.com**

Mail: Steve Weiss
        Executive Editor
        New Riders Publishing
        201 West 103rd Street
        Indianapolis, IN 46290 USA

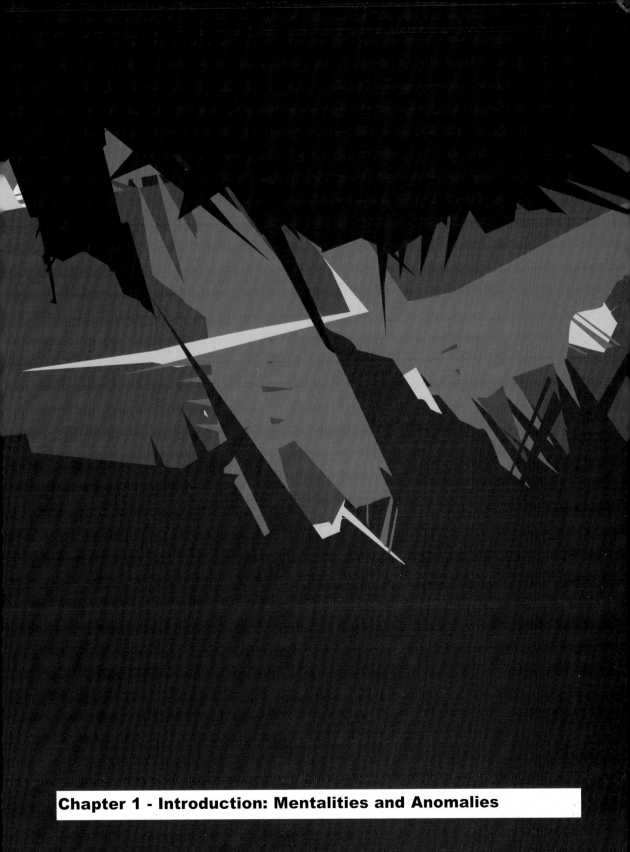

Chapter 1 - Introduction: Mentalities and Anomalies

Mentalities are ways of thinking: a philosophy or a set of constructs or beliefs that guide our rational thought. Anomalies defy our beliefs: An anomaly is something different, something abnormal, or something not easily classified. They are the wormholes in the universe of life experience; as an artist I have found that the most useful mentalities make room for as many anomalies as possible.

Most of the time I'm very confused.

The Power of Confusion

I grew up in Littleton, Colorado. Where I live now is in the state of confusion—a place I'm proud to be.

When I tell people I don't know what I'm doing, they say politely, "Oh, that is very conceptual. Would you like to fly out to speak at a conference?" I have spent much of the past year traveling all over the world just to confess that I have no idea, at all, what I'm doing—really.

Macromedia flew me to Japan once to lecture about Flash. There was a convenience store next to my hotel—a good thing, I thought, because I have a bit of a sweet tooth and love candy. One night I went into the store, found the candy aisle, and purchased something that looked to me like Starburst candy. It was squishy, too, like Starburst. I unwrapped one and popped it into my mouth. It tasted like fish!

So I was a little confused. I went back down the aisle and bought another thing that looked like candy, and it too tasted like fish. I bought a bunch of other stuff, only to find out that everything tasted like fish.

You can imagine this now as a Flash animation. A little figure of me in downtown Tokyo—the camera angle is positioned right above my head, and it's pulling back into space as I'm screaming, "Where's my SUGAR? Everything is FISH!!"

In this chapter, and through the rest of this book, we're going to explore the powerful creative forces of confusion. Those things that at first seem to be weaknesses can turn out to be strengths.

My mother gave me this quote once:

> "It is more rewarding to explore than to reach conclusion; more satisfying to wonder than to know; and more exciting to search than to stay put."

I've personally tried to carry this idea with me through my life.

When I was a kid, I went into my parents' kitchen and looked into a cupboard and found a box of food coloring. I read what was printed on the side of the box: It said, "Non-Toxic." So I took one of the bottles, unscrewed the cap, tilted my head back, and put a drop of food coloring into each of my eyes.

For about 20 seconds, the whole world was *red*.

In my college years I was doing oil paintings on paper, and one day I wondered what would happen if I set my paintings on fire. I was working with two different oil-based resins, and I discovered that when heat was applied, the resins would crack against each other and create interesting textures on the paper.

I started baking my paintings. I would paint on paper, using the two resins, then heat my oven to 450 degrees and slide my painting in on a cookie tray. I would let it heat up for seven or ten minutes, rotating the artwork now and then so the paper wouldn't really catch on fire but just heat up enough to make the cracks.

Next, I would take black oil paint and rub the whole painting black. Then I would take a dry cloth and wipe off the black paint. This would remove the top layer of the paint, but the black color would seep and settle into the cracks. I found that I could paint really modern images and yet make them look like paintings that were 500 years old.

Now, I'm not suggesting that you personally endanger your own life or your own home to work with Flash. (But if you try the thing with the food coloring—and I know some of you will—please be sure to email me from *Praystation.com* about your experience.)

The real lesson is that *not understanding is okay.* I don't know all the answers. No one does. I had to put red food coloring into my eyes to find out what would happen. I had to set my paintings on fire to observe the effect. In all of our mistakes and failures, we can discover great things.

If I ever truly understood all I do with Flash, or with my life in general, I'd probably quit—because that would mean I had lost interest in exploring all the things Flash can do if I push it. No offense to Macromedia, but I have really tried to bring Flash to its knees. Really break it. Slam it. Crashed my computer. It's only in breaking things—in the anomalies—that I find the accidents that in the end become techniques.

What Can Art Teach Commerce?

By reading this book I hope you will be encouraged to discover inspiration in anomalies wherever you find them. Early in my career, I wanted to be a children's book illustrator. One of the books I collected then, and still treasure now, is *The Mysteries of Harris Burdick* by Chris Van Allsburg.

The book is a bunch of wonderfully creative drawings, each with a title and a one-word sentence that contains a bare snippet of story. According to the author, the drawings were given to him by a friend, one Peter Wender, and created by a man named Harris Burdick. Wender related that Burdick had presented him with the drawings as publishing samples and said that he had written and drawn a complete story for each one. Burdick also said he would come back the next day with the completed storybooks.

Days went by. Weeks went by. Years went by, but Harris Burdick was never heard from again. So Van Allsburg and Wender decided to publish the collection as a book. One page, for example, might show a drawing of a little boy and a harp in the foreground sitting on a rock. The caption is: *"Oh, it's true," he thought. "It's really true."* This book is given to children, who are invited to flip through, pick out a picture, and make up their own story or finish what seems to be started. Who is the boy? And what's with the harp?

As an adult, you realize that Harris Burdick never existed; Van Allsburg did the drawings himself and created a false story—a concept for a book that is all about imagination.

The Seven Chairs. The fifth chair wound up in France.
This must have resonance for anyone who ever went to Catholic school.

The Mysteries of Harris Burdick was an early inspiration for *my* web site work. These sites explore sound, design, and interactions, and they present ideas that viewers can finish. Like Van Allsburg's picture book, this web site work becomes what the viewer will make of it.

These web sites also get about 200 emails every day. Most of them, I am pleased to report, are variations on, *"What the hell IS this?"*

So, what does commerce have to learn from art?

I have a studio that sometimes produces work for commercial web sites. I have clients that come in and say: "On the web, we only have two seconds to capture someone's attention. What can you do?"

One thing I can do is point to my stats from the server log files from *these web sites*. The average users spend 30 minutes, and when they're done, they email me, asking to know if they've *missed* anything.

Some site visitors take screen shots, mail me the screen shots, and write, "Am I close?" or, "Here's where I put it—is this the right combination to unlock the rest of the content?"

I am intentionally creating a digital black hole—a site that offers questions but doesn't give out any answers. I have made hundreds and hundreds of people confused, and in that confusion I've created an interesting space and a provocative experience for anyone who logs on.

This is, of course, exactly the kind of deeply involving and richly interactive experience that site visitors and corporate clients seek from the web. At my studio, what we do is try to pull ideas like this into our work and create experiences that are a little more interesting.

Theater of the Web

I didn't have a TV for a long while. Eventually I got one (which I still use mostly to play video games and run DVDs), but one night I turned on my television and saw what looked like a news anchorman.

I was just about to change the channel when he intoned: "Should Bob die?" And then, "Log on to our web site and vote if Bob should die."

I froze. This was intense—so much viewer responsibility. Was Bob going to die? Would he be allowed to live?

I kept watching until the newsman came back and said: "Eighty percent of you voted to say Bob should die." And at that moment I realized that something entirely new was happening to the group entertainment experience.

For much of human history, live theater was the most important part of society's entertainment. This isn't just what's on Broadway today, but it was at Shakespeare's Globe in the sixteenth century and Roman forums in 500 BC. Everyone dressed in their best and cruised on down to see a presentation, a story, a show. The experience was interactive: thumbs up, thumbs down, applause, boos and hisses, leaving at intermission if it turned out to be a bore. The performers would constantly make changes to keep the audience coming back.

Time has progressed, and this group experience is falling by the wayside. Most of us don't see a live theater presentation even once a year. Movie theaters, the more "modern" form of interactive group viewing, are less important, too, now that we can watch films privately and comfortably in our living rooms, alone with our DVDs, our big flat screens, and Surround-Sound.

The story of Bob revealed that the contemporary audience was ready to go beyond the fringe of an anonymous but only passive viewing of a show. People still desire an interactive group experience. They want to realize the moment when what they do and how they feel will actually matter—or at least make an impact on what will happen next. And here comes a medium that will let people have their privacy, but also give them a voice. Log on to an interactive web site where your point of view will be tabulated; your action will affect the results; you will be heard.

Bob's tragic adventure did have some technical flaws as an entertainment experience. To participate, you started in one medium (television) then had to turn to and log onto another medium (your computer). To get the results of your participation and to find out what happened, you had to run back to the original medium (television). But this is changing, too.

The interactive capability of the Internet is going to be the most important medium for society's next group entertainment experience. Time will tell to what extent this medium will evolve. The audience will be global, and it is eagerly waiting.

I choose Flash as a tool because it has the most possibilities for design, movement, sound, and interactivity in this new medium. It's exciting because we will get to change and evolve the medium while we work with this tool as artists, designers, and developers.

You Can Do It

A surprising number of people I've met seem to have the impression that the *Praystation* web site (**www.praystation.com**) is the product of a team of people. There is no team. It's just me—just one guy. It is true that on commercial projects, teams need to be assembled. But for personal, experimental work, you don't need a team. Anybody reading this book now, or anyone viewing the *Praystation* web site, can learn to do what I do.

All it really takes is passion and determination. Another designer I identify with, cartoonist Joe Shields (**www.joecartoon.com**), used to work in a corporate studio. At the end of the day, he and his coworkers would go home. They would perhaps watch TV or just go to sleep, and the next day would come in again. But Joe would get off work, go home, and spend four to six hours on his home computer doing the same exact thing he did during the day—but on work he did for himself. And his passion and determination did not pass unnoticed.

It's a lot of work—for all of us. I didn't just wake up one day and become an artist. When I was an art student at Pratt, there were the times I was nearly evicted, living on Kraft Macaroni and Cheese and Top Ramen noodles. I've crashed and burned but stuck with it.

The Truth About Foundations

So what's your mentality? What's your philosophy? What are you thinking about? What kind of foundation do you have to lay down a body of work?

For a long time, I believed that a foundation was something that came from the past. And in many schools, this is still how art is taught: You are presented with the works and artists of the past to be used as the base or foundation for what will some day be your own innovative work.

Now, I believe that foundation is something that we carry along with us in the moment. Our foundations are not what's been dug up from the past but are all the life experiences we are constantly and inevitably updating and adding on to.

Foundations can be stable, but they can never be static. If you build a building, you can't just construct it and let it be. Unless you perform maintenance updates—replace the roof, repaint the bricks, and so on—the building will eventually crumble due to the work of external forces over time.

The life span of art on the Internet is microscopically short compared to the life of a building. There is a web site that I visit often, one I consider a pioneering work of graphic design. But the creator has not updated his site in two years. When I log on, I already know what I will see, how it will load, and how the interactions will result. I feel sad because it is like looking at a beautiful, dead corpse. The foundation is dead because nothing has changed.

The *Praystation* web site is updated as often as once a day. Why? Because if I stop maintaining the foundations, the experience will die. Visitors will learn what to expect; nothing will be interesting anymore. Another site, *Dreamless* (**www.dreamless.com**), was a community site that was updated constantly by the three or four thousand people who participated in that site. If we can create a world by ourselves, it is up to us to keep that world alive.

Praystation, in particular, is time-based. It represents techniques I've laid down over the past year, though this is not so much for your convenience as it is for mine. I can look back and see what was developed over a period of time, revisit topics, and find ways to do things differently. *Praystation 2002* is evolving as something quite different, although it takes parts of the previous work and rearranges them for new experiences.

As you go through this book, you may wish to view portions of the *Praystation* site that bring to life the animations that illustrate the projects described (for such is the limitation of the printed page). Like the book, the tutorials on the web site should be considered at best only a small portion of the foundation you are adding onto each day for your own art.

When you begin building a visual experience on the screen, you lay down a foundation of parameters based entirely on your own decisions. The foundation suddenly exists in the moment, and you are free to manipulate, extend, and build upon this. Whenever you create a foundation that is unique to the project, you're also building a foundation for further exploration and the next projects. Ideally, you will also be participating in a collaborative discussion with other designers and developers. This work is never finished; the foundation is continually morphing and extending every time someone says, "Hey, but did you know it could do this?"

A Word About Standards

There are books out there about web standards. This isn't one of them.

A lot of people out there want to tell you that things should be a certain way on the web so that every user can see them. I agree with standards—but only up to a certain point. If a large part of your commercial audience reads books, then yes, you can put the information in a book to appeal to that large base of users. But on the web, we should blur the technical assumptions just that little bit more if it means the result will be something amazing. Perhaps the target audience at first will be only a very small, very select group of viewers. But we and they will help evolve and change the medium. If we don't do it, who will?

As developers, designers, and artists, we shouldn't assume that the general public is idiotic. Instead, we should try to evolve the medium by building intuitive systems that educate the user—not design down to the level we think the users can handle.

I have written this book to help you in three ways:

- To show where I get my own ideas
- To give you analogies that will help you tackle certain design problems you may come across
- To provide you with a useful syntax and some tutorials that will help you begin building your own creative worlds with Flash

Once Upon a Forest

Maruto
CELESTIAL ARCHITECT

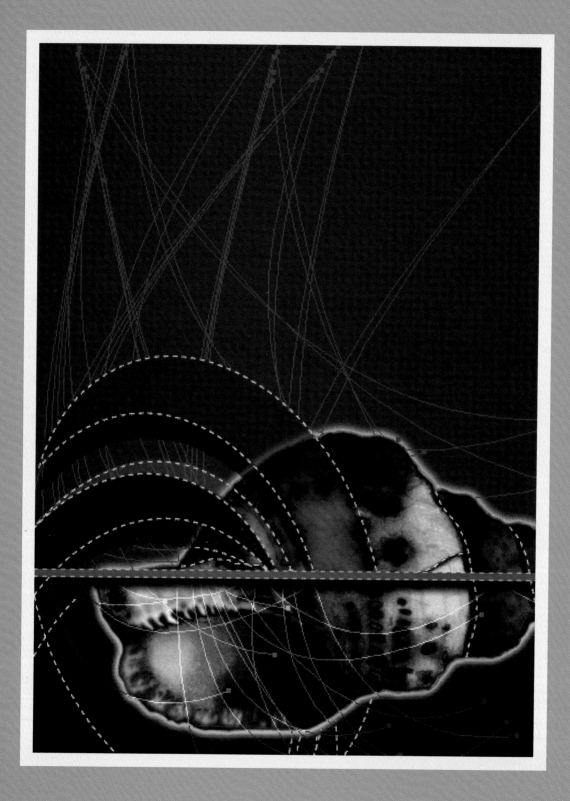

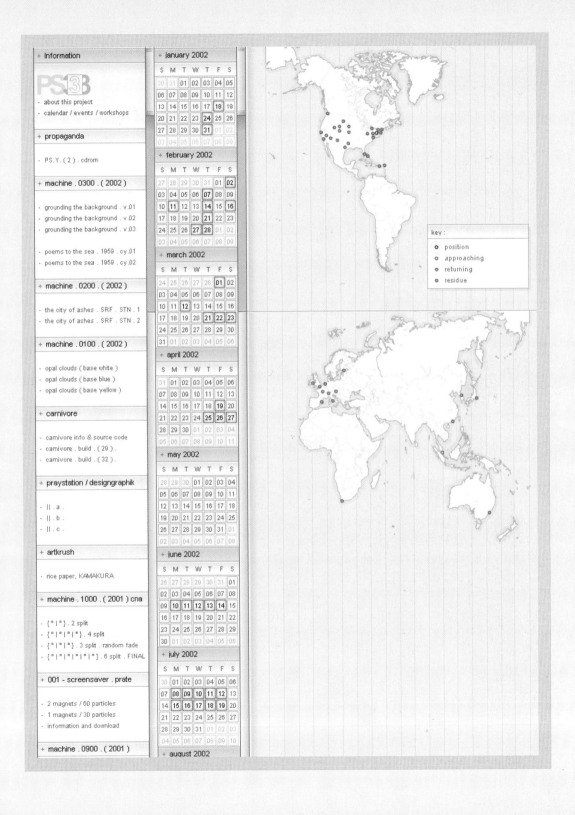

+ Information

PS3B

- about this project
- calendar / events / workshops

+ propaganda

- P.S.Y. (2) . cdrom

+ machine . 0300 . (2002)

- grounding the background . v .01
- grounding the background . v .02
- grounding the background . v .03

- poems to the sea . 1959 . cy .01
- poems to the sea . 1959 . cy .02

+ machine . 0200 . (2002)

- the city of ashes . SRF . STN . 1
- the city of ashes . SRF . STN . 2

+ machine . 0100 . (2002)

- opal clouds (base white)
- opal clouds (base blue)
- opal clouds (base yellow)

+ carnivore

- carnivore info & source code
- carnivore . build . (29) .
- carnivore . build . (32) .

+ praystation / designgraphik

- || . a .
- || . b .
- || . c .

+ artkrush

- rice paper, KAMAKURA

+ machine . 1000 . (2001) cna

- { " | " } . 2 split
- { " | " | " | " } . 4 split
- { " | " | " } . 3 split . random fade
- { " | " | " | " | " } . 6 split . FINAL

+ 001 - screensaver . prate

- 2 magnets / 60 particles
- 1 magnets / 30 particles
- information and download

+ machine . 0900 . (2001)

+ january 2002

S	M	T	W	T	F	S
30	31	01	02	03	04	05
06	07	08	09	10	11	12
13	14	15	16	17	18	19
20	21	22	23	24	25	26
27	28	29	30	31	01	02
03	04	05	06	07	08	09

+ february 2002

S	M	T	W	T	F	S
27	28	29	30	31	01	02
03	04	05	06	07	08	09
10	11	12	13	14	15	16
17	18	19	20	21	22	23
24	25	26	27	28	01	02
03	04	05	06	07	08	09

+ march 2002

S	M	T	W	T	F	S
24	25	26	27	28	01	02
03	04	05	06	07	08	09
10	11	12	13	14	15	16
17	18	19	20	21	22	23
24	25	26	27	28	29	30
31	01	02	03	04	05	06

+ april 2002

S	M	T	W	T	F	S
31	01	02	03	04	05	06
07	08	09	10	11	12	13
14	15	16	17	18	19	20
21	22	23	24	25	26	27
28	29	30	01	02	03	04
05	06	07	08	09	10	11

+ may 2002

S	M	T	W	T	F	S
28	29	30	01	02	03	04
05	06	07	08	09	10	11
12	13	14	15	16	17	18
19	20	21	22	23	24	25
26	27	28	29	30	31	01
02	03	04	05	06	07	08

+ june 2002

S	M	T	W	T	F	S
26	27	28	29	30	31	01
02	03	04	05	06	07	08
09	10	11	12	13	14	15
16	17	18	19	20	21	22
23	24	25	26	27	28	29
30	01	02	03	04	05	06

+ july 2002

S	M	T	W	T	F	S
30	01	02	03	04	05	06
07	08	09	10	11	12	13
14	15	16	17	18	19	20
21	22	23	24	25	26	27
28	29	30	31	01	02	03
04	05	06	07	08	09	10

+ august 2002

key :

- position
- approaching
- returning
- residue

Part I - Understanding Flash

Chapter 2 - Timelines and Foundation Environments

When you first open Flash, you begin to create the foundation environments for your creative work. This chapter covers some key principles, such as the concept of the Stage and the idea of Timelines, along with my suggested methods of establishing an organizational structure for your work to help make the art flow more easily and intuitively.

The documentation for Flash uses some terminology that is too abstract to be useful. The creative assets of Movie Clips, Buttons, and Graphics are all called Symbols, for example. I prefer to simply call these assets *Objects*— but more on why later.

The *Stage* is the term used for the screen area where animations can be played and is an important concept for our Theater of the Web. A Stage implies stage actions and audience interactions, which can get you beyond the idea that you are merely creating flat images for a flat screen. Think of your creative elements not as representational "Symbols," but as Objects you create that are completely in your power. My approach is that I am a director and my Objects are my "actors." I'm going to ask my actors to do various things on the Stage. What is most important to the principle of the Stage is that the acting, in response to my stage directions, is going to take place *over time*.

Understanding Timelines

Live theater is a useful analogy to comprehend the importance of time and Timelines in Flash. Like live theater, Flash can only go forward in time. If you look at the playhead, (which runs across the Timeline that appears onscreen to show the unfolding of the animation sequence), you'll notice that animations always start at 1 and then go forward. The problem I see in looking at other people's Flash Movies is that most only use Flash for animations that go forward in time.

You can make Flash go backward; that is, you can make it appear that an action is going backward (Chapter 8, "The Perfect Fade," explains how to do this). But I don't see many people doing more than simply creating Movies that go forward in time. This is a limitation in mindframe—neither a limitation of the medium nor a limitation of the tool.

Think of television, which has the concept of instant replay. Now think of a videocassette recorder. If I have some friends over and I put a tape in my VCR, I know the movie will last a time "distance" of perhaps two hours. But I can push the Play button, and we might watch perhaps only the first 15 minutes of the movie. Then I could pause it, and I might turn to the people in the room with me and say, "Well, what should we do next?" Given the limits of VCR technology, our only real options would be to show the scenes in reverse or fast forward. Or I could hit Play again and continue to run the rest of the movie. Or I turn the whole thing off and we could all listen to music instead.

If a VCR were truly interactive, as the web is, at this point we could go into the story and, as a group, affect the result—change the story, or even vote if Bob should die. But most of us don't even take advantage of the limited functional options available in a VCR; we just press Play. In much the same way, a Flash animation is based in time, and its time can be manipulated; users can stop it, and users can start playing it again. But most of us don't explore the more extensive interactive possibilities this can create in a Flash Movie.

In Chapter 3, "Hierarchies and Object Relations," for example, I will be talking about Movie Clips. The wonderful thing about Movie Clips is that they have their own individual Timelines, completely independent of the main Timeline (also called the *root* or *level 0* Timeline.) My main or root Timeline may start at 1 on the playhead and extend until 100. But I can actually have the playhead move forward and program it to stop at 50. Then I can give a stage direction to play a Movie Clip—that is, I can program Flash to find a Movie Clip that I've named Explosion (for example) and play out its Timeline at that point.

The program will find the Movie Clip, Explosion, and start to play Explosion's independent Timeline. Let's say this is an animation of an explosion, and it runs from 1 to 25 on its own Timeline.

When the explosion has been viewed, the program can back up to the root Timeline—remember we paused at 50—and start playing that again, 51, 52, and so on up to 100. This is one way to manipulate time in Flash: running one Timeline, pausing, playing another time, then going back to the root Timeline, perhaps stopping again and then asking another piece of time to play backward.

So when you think about Timelines, think not only of moving forward, but of pausing, then possibly reversing certain actions.

A Few Words About Scenes

As just discussed, Flash animations run along a root Timeline. Individual Movie Clips have their own Timelines, which can be independent of the root Timeline, and the root Timeline can be made up of Scenes.

The nature of Flash is that whenever you open the program, it always defaults to a new scene, Scene1. It will also stitch Scenes together automatically along the Timeline: If Scene1 plays from Frame 1 to Frame 10, it will be followed by Scene2, which might run from Frame 1 until Frame 50; then it plays a Scene3, which might run from 1 to 1000.

Scenes are good because they can run independently or sequentially, which allows you to control the pacing of your Flash movie. You can also jump from Scene to Scene, to create variations in pacing.

But Scenes are bad if you want to maintain continuity throughout a Flash movie. A real world example would be a web site animation with a few active elements that appear on every web page: For example, a navigation bar (navbar), a corporate logo, or a copyright notice. Because Flash assumes each new scene will be created, on a bare Stage with a blank Timeline, any element that is global to all scenes will have to be copied, cut, and pasted into every new page.

The laborious way to solve this problem would be to copy all the scenes repeatedly, strip away all those elements that are not global, and then add the new content. The only practical way to handle the problem is to design all the global material first and lay it in before you've even started thinking about the really creative content.

So I never use Scenes. Never. Ever.

Setup and Modifying Setup

Your creative foundation is based upon your understanding of how the tool will work for you. Flash is a program that provides an artist with a great many choices—beyond simply selecting between object-based and cel-based animations. There is usually more than one way to get where you want to go in Flash. It should come as no surprise to you that the first thing I do when I open Flash is to modify the program.

The setup for Flash MX involves a completely different orientation to the program.

The major enhancement is the *Property Inspector*, an information palette that is contextual and will change according to the work activities you are doing. For example, if I grab the Rectangle tool, this palette will show some input fields so I can specify the rectangle's color and size. If I choose the Type tool, the palette will show information relating to the kind of type I've selected, and if I choose the Align tool, the Property Inspector will show the screen coordinates that correspond to the movements of the Align tool's arrow.

In Flash 4 and 5, each of these tools had its own palette, although they could be rearranged on a work screen. By combining these into a single, contextual palette, the Property Inspector clears that bit of clutter and offers a slight improvement to your work speed.

When you run Flash MX for the first time, you'll get Macromedia's default layout, which has the toolbar on the left and some of the palettes, such as Color, on the right. The Property Inspector sits at the bottom of the screen.

For my own work, I prefer to rearrange these panels slightly, and I would like to suggest some modifications to you. To modify the panel layouts from the default setup, pull down the Window menu from the top toolbar and select Panel Sets.

This selection offers you six different suggested preset panel sets, three for developers, and three for designers. Well, I like as much control as possible in my working environment, so I've ignored all the presets and made my own.

You can drag all the panels around and dock them wherever you want to. I prefer to have all of my palettes in one central area—no point in moving from one side of the screen to another just to mix a color. So I moved all mine to a strip along the left side of my Stage work area: the toolbar, the Info palette, the Align tool, the Color Mixer, and the Color Swatches.

I put my Property Inspector at the top of the screen, next to the other navigation features. These are my preferences. You can customize your work area to suit your own method.

My hardware configuration is to run dual monitors. I run my palettes, my Property Inspector, and my Stage on one monitor, and I use the other monitor solely for my Library and for the Actions window. All my tools are on the left and all my code is on the right. I think it's well worth the extra few hundred dollars because it makes the process run, oh, ten trillion times faster!

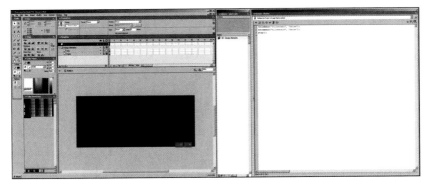

Built for speed: This panel layout puts the tools to the left of the Stage, and the Library and Actions window to the right (on a second monitor).

If you have the resources to get two monitors, consider it. Once you've assembled all your assets for a movie, and all that's left is to write the code. You can do this easily in the Actions window and you'll have an uncluttered, full view of the Stage and the Objects you are working with.

If you are working on one monitor, however, there has been a great improvement in screen flexibility with Flash MX. Every single one of the menus has a turn-down arrow—Mac users sometimes call it a windowshade—that rolls up the menu and makes it go away. I would suggest that you drag your Actions window down to the bottom of your work area. When you're not writing code, you can just minimize it by clicking the minimizer button in the window's frame. When you are ready to write code, you can just roll it up into view, and it will still be somewhat less obstructive.

While you're in Panel Sets, you can select Save Panel Layout to make your customized layout the default. When you click on this, a dialog box will ask you to name the layout. So go ahead and type in **My Default Layout** or whatever you wish.

I also prefer to modify the Movie Properties in Flash. For example, I often alter the frame rate. When you click on the Stage in Flash MX, by default the Property Inspector will automatically show you the Movie attributes you are working with. It will show you the size of your movie in pixels and give you the defaults for Publish, Background, and Frame Rate. You can also access Movie Properties by pressing Ctrl+M (or, for a Macintosh, Cmd+M).

Among the Movie Properties you will notice that the default—for anytime you open the program to create a new project—is 12 frames per second (12fps).

Now I personally don't think 12fps is good. I think it's limiting. So what I do—and what I would suggest to you—is to modify the frame rate to 24fps, which is the same frame rate used in 35mm film moviemaking.

Increasing the frame rate will give your Flash movies a little more pickup and make them look a lot more like film. I find a rate of 24fps is useful when I want something to look like it's moving slowly—I can extend the movement in time. If I want things to move faster, I can shorten the animations on my Timelines.

Objects

Macromedia refers to the most creative assets in Flash as Symbols. I prefer to use the term *Objects* for the three things that are obviously Objects to me: Movie Clips, Buttons, and Graphics.

I teach my students to think of these as Objects, ideally not as representations but as three-dimensional Objects on the Stage because it's a way to more quickly grasp methods of manipulating between levels when you are creating multiple Timelines and doing animations that are Object-Oriented.

Objects can be put within other Objects. They're like cardboard boxes that can be put into larger cardboard boxes. By dragging and clicking, you can put a Button into a Graphic. You can put a Graphic into a Movie Clip. You can put a Movie Clip into a Button. Any Object can be placed in any other Object. Boxes in boxes.

3 dimensional objects

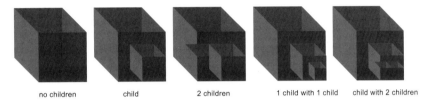

| no children | child | 2 children | 1 child with 1 child | child with 2 children |

Try to think of everything you create in Flash as three-dimensional objects. Like empty boxes, boxes can be put in other boxes. This will help you quickly understand parent/child relationships.

This very simple idea is the basis for some easy and elegantly useful projects, such as the One Button Trick (see Chapter 7, "Movie Clips as Buttons and the One Button Trick"), which has many real-world applications in web site design.

But this is also the basis for some very complex animations, which involve writing code within Objects and letting these instructions play out through many levels of Object hierarchy.

Once you start putting Objects within Objects, you can monitor the effects of each Object and wield complete control. As separate Objects, they can contain separate code that can be isolated and debugged without affecting the rest of the activities that are going on along the Timelines.

An analogy I use with my students uses an animation of drivers in cars. In this case, the Stage is now a parking lot. I can create as Objects three different cars—red, green, and blue—and designate each car as a different Movie Clip. Inside each "car" I can put other Objects: I can put in Graphics, and I can put in other Movie Clips that will be the drivers. As Red Driver, Green Driver, and Blue Driver are Movie Clips, I can give separate code to each of the drivers with the directions about how they will drive their cars around the parking lot. Now remember, as Movie Clips, each driver also has its own, independent Timeline. So that's where each driver's coding can be placed.

But in Flash MX, perhaps 90 percent of the time, the most efficient way to write code will be to write it on the root Timeline.

A big difference between Flash 5 and Flash MX is that we no longer have to attach code to Movie Clips. We can now, very quickly and efficiently, write all the code on the root Timeline and address all of our Movie Clips more directly. Directions that in previous versions had to be given as attached code using onClipEvents, such as enterFrame, which directs a clip to play a frame in a continuous loop, can now be written much more simply and elegantly as code on the root Timeline.

In the cars, drivers, and parking lots analogy, I would generally give all the code to the driver Movie Clips. The car Movie Clips were by comparison inanimate Objects. There are probably about ten percent of situations where this still makes sense, when you are writing generic code. But the cars can now be directed by a force beyond their drivers—by code that's been written on the root Timeline.

The Importance of Expert Mode

ActionScript is a programming language unique to Flash, and we write our ActionScript in an Object Actions window, which is basically a text editor. Add to your foundation by considering that there are two ways of inputting the code you will want to write.

The default mode when you open Flash 5 or Flash MX is the *Normal mode*. Normal mode assumes you will be picking the ActionScript from a menu tree on the left side of the screen. It will add them to the editor window on the right side of the screen and provide you with an input menu on the bottom to affect the values of certain actions and functions that you will be calling up.

Normal mode is image-based and visual; that is, if you want to work in this mode, you will be using three menu windows and will double-click to grab items from a drop-down menu, input the code in another window, and make value changes someplace else.

Expert mode does not rely on menus. Expert mode assumes you know what you are doing, and it allows you to input code just by typing it in.

Throughout the rest of this book we are going to be discussing ActionScript as written code in Expert mode. Why? Because this is the most efficient way and most correct way to write code in Flash.

True, the program supports both. Normal mode remains for the artists and developers who prefer a visual method for writing ActionScript and don't like the idea of typing in stuff like programmers do.

Over the course of the tutorials in this book you will see a lot of written code—in Expert mode. Don't even try to do the work if you only want to use the drop-down menus. Expert mode blows the lid off Normal mode's capabilities: It is the fastest way to create with Flash.

The only trick to it is that the commands are case-sensitive, and part of your foundation is being familiar with typing common commands and directions where words may be smashed together but controlled by the capital letters at the start of each word. At first, you may find this slower than working with the more visual style of Normal mode. But stick with it, and in a month your stuff is going to *rock*.

To put yourself into Expert mode, click with your cursor on the right-corner box of the Actions Frame window when you open Flash. The dialog box will then ask you what mode you prefer: Normal or Expert.

(The shortcut in Flash MX is **Ctrl+Shift+N** for Normal mode; **Ctrl+Shift+E** for Expert.)

Movie Clips, Buttons, and Graphics

A Movie Clip, as we've mentioned, can have its own Timeline that operates independently of the root Timeline. You can also "talk to" a Movie Clip once you give it an *instance name*. You can give it a command and tell it to do things on your Stage as if it were an actor and you were giving it stage directions.

In older versions of Flash, you couldn't give a Button an instance name, so you couldn't talk to a Button. What's new in Flash MX is that you can give a Button an instance name so it can be talked to and directed as if it were a Movie Clip.

Buttons are generally reactive to other things that will be happening on your Stage. Buttons enable a computer user or web site viewer to affect or change what happens next on screen. Or, to continue the theater analogy, Buttons allow the members of the audience to call out certain kinds of directions to the actors when they are on the stage. In reaction to directions from the audience, your actors may improvise, but only to the extent that you, the director, have told them to.

One of the biggest changes in Flash MX it that it now gives Movie Clips all of the capabilities claimed by Buttons. For example, we can now give an onPress or onRelease direction to a Movie Clip to prompt a reaction to these movements of a user's mouse. Or we can give a onRollOver direction to a Movie Clip to respond to the rollover of a user's cursor.

This means that in some of the tutorials in this book, we may not create a single Button. In terms of interface functionality, using Movie Clips as Buttons can create a more transparent and perhaps a more exciting interactive experience. Another method—creating "transparent" Buttons—is described in Chapter 7 and has its uses as well.

The benefit of being able to give Buttons an instance name means we can now create Buttons on the fly—for example, to track a user's navigation on a web site. This can make it possible to determine which Buttons in a group have been clicked most often or which elements in a web site are the most attractive to a particular user. These answers, in turn, can set off a customized response by the program. Tracking which Buttons have just been clicked can also prompt some immediate screen feedback: For example, a visual element can get bigger and bigger every time it is clicked.

Graphics still can't be given an instance name or be used the way Movie Clips can. This means that you, as the stage director, can't give a Graphic any directions or tell it what to do. Think of Graphics as scenery and props for your stage. Actors have names; scenery does not. You can tell an actor what to do—give him directions to walk across the stage towards a tree or get into a car. You can't tell a prop tree or prop car on the stage to move. It just can't do that by itself.

The way to get around this, of course, is to rename your Graphic as a Movie Clip. Once it's a Movie Clip, it comes to life to follow your directions. Once we re-identify it under the Movie Clip icon, we can name this bit of scenery Car or Tree and give it an instance name as well. It will now move across the stage (if we give it those directions).

I know what you're thinking. If Movie Clips are more fun than Graphics, why not rename every Graphic as a Movie Clip? Why not make everything you put on screen into a Movie Clip?

The simple answer is that in most animations you will want your actors to act independently of the background scenery. Some stuff really is just background. It doesn't have to move around.

The more complicated answer has to do with the processing capacity of the Flash program and the processing capacity of the computer that will play back your animation. Flash will use all its power to manage the playback of Movie Clips, and the more Movie Clips going on in a Timeline sequence, the harder Flash must work.

Think of Movie Clips as a bunch of little children running around in a nursery school class. They all have names and can be told what to do (more or less). Now imagine the Flash program as a nursery school teacher, in charge of all the children. Flash has to watch them all. Perhaps there are toys in the room as well; Flash doesn't have to watch them nor care about them. They are inanimate Objects, the way Graphics are. Flash doesn't have to pay attention to Graphics and so can focus its processing efforts to make sure the Movie Clips are running around in the right way.

If you'd like to see what happens when Movie Clips run amok, take a look at the sample animation engine in Machine 1100 (2000) on *Praystation.com*. In this engine, there are two crosshairs: One is following commands for random action; the second has been programmed to chase the first at a slight time lag. With every cycle, the engine draws a line between both crosshairs.

While at first this seems simply a vision of one line chasing another, every initial line drawn is a newly created Movie Clip. Because each line is a Movie Clip, Flash has to keep thinking about them, even though they look static on the screen. As Movie Clips, they may be called upon to take a new stage direction, and Flash has to keep monitoring each of their individual Timelines along with the root Timeline, spending its processing power on a task that grows exponentially as the Movie Clips are continually created and duplicated.

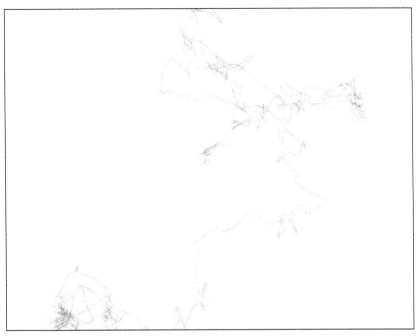

A chase scene with moving, replicating lines that are Movie Clips. (*Praystation.com,* MACHINE 1100 [2000])

If you watch this animation for about two minutes, you'll notice the chasing action seems to slow down. What's actually happening is the processing speed is slowing down. Watch too long, and you may crash your computer. Your CPU can't handle it. It's as if someone suddenly began adding more and more children to a nursery class—first ten children, then a hundred, then a thousand. The teacher soon couldn't give sufficient attention.

But imagine if more and more toys are put into the room. Things might get crowded, but the teacher wouldn't care. All the teacher has to worry about are the live children running around.

There is a way to get around the problem of too many Movie Clips running at the same time. In the same way you can program the duplication of a Movie Clip, you can also command the deletion of a Movie Clip at a certain point in time. In other words, you can tell a Movie Clip to kill itself in a timely fashion, and it will depart from the Stage, to free up processing power for other tasks.

If you look at the Machine 0100 (2001) sample animation engine on *Praystation.com*, you can see how this problem is solved: Some of the earlier lines start fading away. In this variation, all these Movie Clips, even as they are created and duplicated, have been given a temporary life expectancy. If Flash has to bring to life and manage a hundred Movie Clips at a time in this animation, it can keep going without crashing because the earlier Movie Clips are removing themselves.

A similar chase scene, with lines that are Movie Clips that fade and remove themselves from the screen. (*Praystation.com*, MACHINE 0100 [2001])

Movie Clip Naming Convention

When you create Movie Clips in Flash MX, you will notice that the Property Inspector will bug you to immediately give it an instance name. A simple change to the way you give instance names adds a new level of functionality here.

In older versions, if you created a Movie Clip of a pink-colored box and called it "Pink Box," you might give it an instance name of "pinkBox" as well. Then if you were writing code, you might start out like this:

```
_root.pinkBox
```

But in Flash MX, you can work a little quicker if you use a naming convention that will identify Movie Clips as distinguished from other elements.

What I've been doing in Flash MX is writing Movie Clip instance names like this:

```
pinkBox_mc
```

The first part of this convention is specific to the Object, a pink box. The second part, _mc, reminds me that this is indeed a Movie Clip. Now, if I'm writing code and I start by writing

```
_root.pinkBox_mc
```

as soon as I type in that period mark (.), something very interesting happens on the screen. The contextual menu pops up and lists all of the attributes that are available to Movie Clips within ActionScript. Remember, however, that you must type **_mc.** for this to work; just appending **_mc** to your Object name does not call the menu.

The Library

I consider the Library to be the most important and valuable aspect of Flash. I'm really hard-core about organizing and using the Library to its utmost potential. And yet I open a lot of other people's Movies and look at their Library—nine times out of ten, I can see it is a neglected tool.

Let's look at the basic principle. If I physically walk into a real library, the library I am visiting might have perhaps 10,000 books. All these books are individual "Objects"—all separate things, not related at all. There could be one book on Shakespeare and another book on Dante. These are two separate Objects.

So I'm in this library with 10,000 books. I can walk over to a shelf and pull out one book and set it down on an empty table. The table is my "Stage." When I set the book down, it is now an Object on my Stage. I may walk to another shelf in the stacks, pull out another book, and put that on the table as well. I can do this a few more times, and perhaps I'll end up with nine books on my table—nine Objects on my Stage. There may be 10,000 books in the library, but only nine on my Stage.

Let's think ahead now to the process of exporting a Movie from Flash. Understand that we can put things into the Flash Library, but we don't have to use them all. You could literally have 10,000 Objects in your Flash Library, but when it comes time to export your Movie, you will only export nine. You are only going to use those Objects that you pulled out.

You also understand that your Library can contain and store not only Objects (which can be Movie Clips, Buttons, or Graphics) but also other assets, such as audio files. These can be taken out and put on the Stage as well, for exporting later to the real world.

Setting Up Your Library

A good Library is organized so you can find things quickly when you need them. Let me show you how I set up my own Library onscreen and how I name and file Objects as I work.

To open the Library, choose Library from the Window menu or use the keyboard shortcut: Ctrl+L (on Macintosh, Cmd+L).

Once open, you'll see a little window on screen. The top part is gray—that's the part where you can preview what's in an Object. Below that is a list of the Objects you'll put in your Library. On the right side you will see a menu for Options. Click that, and you'll see there are lots of things we can do with the Library.

The top two functions are those you will be using the most: New Symbol and New Folder.

In the Library we have the ability to name our Objects. Flash will automatically alphabetize any names. Anything that starts with A is going to be at the top of your Library file, and anything that starts with Z is going to be near the bottom. You can immediately see the problems inherent in naming your Objects alphabetically.

Flash puts numerics above the alphabet, however. The number 0, or 10, or 100 or even 1000 are always going to be above A. This provides a way to organize assets and work within projects, which allows you to move swiftly and competently through the entire process.

Consider a movie: First, we have the opening credits, which has the title, director's name, and so on. Then, there is an intro—the introduction of the characters and setting of the mood. After that, scenes will build to some kind of climax—perhaps it will be a big fight scene—and then there will be a denouement, a decline, and finally the ending credits.

I want to name things in the order that they happen. So I use folders, and create new folders for each of those movie elements that will happen in time.

To create a folder, simply click New Folder in the Options menu. You can also click a little folder icon in the bottom left of the window. You will then see an empty folder called Untitled Folder 1.

Click again and you'll get a folder called Untitled Folder 2 and so on. So you can see that Flash itself is already trying to organize folders for you.

The next step is to name the folders by clicking on the name bar below the folder. The first folder I will name by typing **01**, then a space, then a hyphen, then a space again, then the words **Opening Credits**. And then I'll hit the Return key. For example:

> My first folder is 01 - Opening Credits
> My second folder is 02 - Introduction

Notice I am organizing *numerically* here. I can put all my Objects that deal with opening credits into the Opening Credits folder, and I can put all my animations, pictures, and music that pertain to the introduction into the Introduction folder, and so on.

This may sound painfully simple and basic, but I am continually surprised how few developers take this path. The advantage is considerable. Let's say there is a mistake in my opening credits: I play the animation for a client, and it becomes apparent the name of the director is spelled wrong. All I have to do is open my Library, double-click the 01 - Opening Credits folder, and see all my assets there.

And I can make the change within minutes—perhaps seconds—because I have organized *even more deeply* within the folder.

To do this yourself, click New Symbol in the Library's Options menu. You will see a submenu for symbol properties. One of these is Name. Well, the default provided is Symbol 1, and that doesn't tell us anything.

The submenu does give us three radio buttons to specify if the Symbol is a Movie Clip, a Button, or a Graphic. Let's say I've created an Object that is a Movie Clip, so the first thing I do is to check Movie Clip.

This Movie Clip belongs to the opening credits: It contains the text graphics that indicate the director, "A Film by James Davis." So I'm going to drag the little Movie Clip icon into the folder named 01 - Opening Credits. Once it's inside, I will name the Symbol for what the Movie Clip contains:

> 01 - director

In this same file I may have:

> 02 - title
> 03 - actor

Organizing your Library with regard to what happens on your Stage within a time sequence is probably the most important discipline to learn as you begin to explore creativity in Flash. Any time you want to make an adjustment to a completed animation—or whenever a client wants you to make an adjustment—you can quickly go to the correct folder, isolate the problem, and make the change. In the preceding example, I would simply open the Library, open the 01 - Opening Credits folder, open the 01 - director file, and make the name change so that it reads James Michael Davis.

Amazingly, some people don't even bother to name anything at all. One time I opened some guy's Library file, and he had just one long, long list—labeled Symbol 1, Symbol 65, Symbol 132, and so on. Flash is such a quick medium that often people don't take the time to organize their work. But the Library will save you—it can be the gatekeeper for your Objects and all other assets.

My advice: Be really insane about organizing the Objects in your Library and use numerics to arrange your assets in the Library according to the order they will happen on your Stage.

Organizing Timelines

All of this insanely minute organization has its counterpart—practically in mirror symmetry—to how we can organize elements of a movie or a Movie Clip within its Timeline.

The older versions of Flash gave us the ability to create layers of Timelines. Now, with Flash MX, we have the added capability to organize these layers into folders as well. I consider this is a tremendous enhancement.

Let's say you have groups of items on your Stage. All of them are on different layers of Timeline; some of them are specific to a certain onscreen element, such as a top navigator bar.

You can now create a general layer of Timeline, and name this layer "01 - navbar." And then you can drag all those navbar-specific layers into this one layer, and close it just like you would close a folder, collapsing it down to a single line.

And if you have arranged all the assets for the navbar in your Library within a folder you've also named 01 - navbar, you will now be able to more easily keep track of all elements in a very streamlined and efficient way, both on and off the Stage.

You also may feel more comfortable when creating your assets directly on the Stage. Let's say that on a single layer of the Timeline, you might draw several assets, for example, a bunch of different boxes or other visual elements. In Flash MX, you have the ability to highlight that layer with your cursor, go into Modify and click on a function called Distribute to Layers (the keyboard shortcut is Ctrl+Shift+D). This will put every single item in that layer on in its own separate layer. At that point, you can work further with each element and start to turn them into Movie Clips, Graphics, or Buttons, gaining another advantage in control and speed.

Remember the Dewey Decimal System? A well-organized Flash Library also uses numerics—in this case to identify folders and their contents.

Chapter 3 - Hierarchies and Object Relationships

Now we've established the notion that we have Objects—our actors on the Stage—and we need to talk to them. But we need to talk to them in an efficient manner and devise some ways so that the audience (web site visitors and other users) can control some of the action and give our cast a few stage directions of their own. This is where we get into the struggle of hierarchies.

Targeting

What I want to say about targeting only concerns the targeting of Timelines, Scenes, Levels, Movie Clips, Variables, and everything else that can have an instance name.

Targeting is how the director "talks to" the actors on the Stage. Targeting is also what you use for navigation controls that may be manipulated by the user or by some random trigger during the playback of the animation.

For example, we can do targeting with Buttons so that users can start or stop Movie Clips anywhere on the Stage. We can use targeting for our own directions to make Movie Clips move along within their own Timeline. We may tell those Movie Clips to play, or we may tell those Movie Clips to go to a certain frame within that clip's independent Timeline and then stop. Or we can go to a certain frame within a Movie Clip's Timeline and start playing it from that point. But you don't have to send the direction to something that is static. The direction can be sent to modify or to set the value of a *variable*, so a screen Object can be responsive while its performing, perhaps responding to a direction that is itself dynamic and is changing as it goes along.

There are three ways to address Objects, which are:

1. _root
2. _parent
3. this

The first method, using the **_root** of the main Stage, is called *absolute targeting*. The second method, using **_parent**, is called *relative addressing*. It facilitates how Objects within Objects can talk to their parent objects—that is, the Objects they are sitting in. The **this** address has no underscore. That's how Objects talk to themselves. Using the **_root**, or absolute targeting, is the most direct way to direct Objects that are on the Stage or Objects that are embedded into other Objects. Thus, if I have a Movie Clip named Renee_mc with a Movie Clip inside it called Lockhart_mc, the command

```
_root.renee_mc.lockhart_mc.gotoAndstop(2)
```

means: Absolutely start from the Stage, absolutely find the Movie Clip called Renee_mc, then find the Movie Clip inside there that is called Lockhart_mc, and go to and stop at Frame 2 in the Timeline of the Lockhart_mc clip.

This is the most direct way, but it's not always the best way to address Movie Clips and other Objects. For one thing, it's not flexible if I want to change it later. If I decided to insert another box between Lockhart_mc and Renee_mc—a new Movie Clip named Alison_mc—I would have to go into my code and insert the middle name in all those lines:

```
_root.renee_mc.alison_mc.lockhart_mc.gotoAndStop(2)
```

I would have to rewrite all my code to insert that one name everywhere.

Relative addressing uses _**parent**. It's most useful for addressing objects that are within objects—for example Movie Clips that reside within Movie Clips (our boxes-within-boxes analogy again). If there is a Movie Clip Lockhart_mc within a Movie Clip Renee_mc, and I want the first Movie Clip to talk to or direct the second, I'd say _**parent**, and it would go up to Renee_mc. The code would look like this:

```
_parent.gotoAndStop(2);
```

In some cases, I'll want a Movie Clip embedded in one object to react to, talk to, or otherwise affect a Movie Clip embedded in a different object. What is the best way to address that second clip?

Let's look at the objects on the Stage in a slightly different way. The theater analogy we've been using assumes that the director is giving instructions to adults. We assume adults are smart. But Objects in Flash aren't that smart. They are really more like children, and the director's role is really more like that of a babysitter—or more precisely, like the teacher in a day care center.

Objects within Objects are child-like in the way they take direction. A child has to mind its own parent, but in the world of Flash, if a child wants to play with another child, it has to first ask its mother—its *parent*—for permission.

Let's say we have two Movie Clips: One is called Adult1_mc, and the other is named Adult2_mc. Inside of Adult1_mc are her children—other Movie Clips named Child1A_mc, Child2A_mc, and Child3A_mc. Inside of Adult2_mc is Child1B_mc. So if Child1A_mc wants to talk to Child1B_mc, then Child1A_mc has to ask his adult (_**parent**), and then the adult (Adult1_mc) has to ask the other adult (Adult2_mc) if Child1B_mc is available to talk to Child1A_mc.

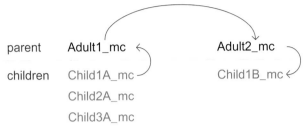

parent	Adult1_mc	Adult2_mc
children	Child1A_mc	Child1B_mc
	Child2A_mc	
	Child3A_mc	

A family of Objects talk amongst themselves.

If I want to do this as a relative address, I can write:

```
_parent._parent.Adult2_mc.Child1B_mc.gotoAndPlay (2);
```

What I'm really saying is: "Go up one, go up one, find Adult2_mc, then go down to Child1B_mc, move to Frame 2, and play."

A more efficient method would be absolute addressing:

```
_root.adult2_mc.Child1B_mc.gotoAndPlay(2);
```

This being the case, you might be tempted to think that relatives are more trouble than they're worth.

On the other hand, let's assume the kids are a bit older now and Child3A_mc has his own Movie Clip child. This "grandchild" is named Grandchild1_mc. If Grandchild1_mc wants to talk to Child2A_mc, he has to ask his own parent, Child3A_mc first. So the coding would be:

```
_parent.child2A_mc.gotoAndPlay(2);
```

This means, "Grandchild1_mc, go up to your parent, who is Child3A_mc, and he will let you talk to Child2A_mc, who will move to Frame 2 and play."

Adult1_mc	Adult2_mc
Child1A_mc	Child1B_mc
Child2A_mc	
parent Child3A_mc	
child Grandchild1_mc	

Grandchild1 talking to Child2A.

The important points are these: First, you build your own foundation more strongly when you keep in mind that there is more than one way to talk to Objects. And second, when we are working and communicating to Objects within Objects, it is useful to remember that while a parent on the Stage can have many children, a child can only have one parent.

The Rigid Hierarchies of Scenes

One of the reasons I dislike using Scenes to build projects is the rigidity in their relationships to each other. In some ways Scenes are tied together far too much, and in other ways they are too stubbornly independent of each other.

When you open up Flash, your screen will show you a blank Timeline at the top and a blank Stage at the bottom. When you have finished working on this part of the file, you can save it all. What you save will be Scene1, and it is the combination of what you've put on the Stage plus the time dimension of how the performance will play out along the Timeline.

Clicking Modify and then Scene opens the scene palette that allows you to create a new Scene. Upon adding a new Scene, you'll be presented with another blank Timeline and its blank Stage. This will be Scene2.

When you export this file, Flash will automatically stitch the two Scenes together for playback. Unless you've put a stop command in there somewhere, when the program finishes playing Scene1, it will automatically begin to play Scene2.

Here are two ways to move from one Scene to another in your projects. The first way is to target your Scene by using the coding commands for next scene:

```
nextScene ();
```

or previous scene:

```
prevScene ();
```

The second way is to target the subsequent Scene by name:

```
gotoAndPlay ("Scene1", 1);
```

This means, "Go to and find the Scene named Scene1 and play it, starting at Frame 1."

But the Objects you can use to do this targeting have been given limitations. The only way you can really create an interactive point is by placing a Button on the Stage. If there is a Button on the Stage in Scene 2, the Button has the option of switching the playback to either the previous Scene or to the very next Scene, or it has the second option of targeting a Scene-specific name. It can call another Scene by name and move the viewer to Scene 3 or Scene 15 if it is activated.

But the Object can *only* be a Button. A Button inside of a Movie Clip or inside of a Graphic does not have the capability to call another Scene by name.

Furthermore (and I really hate this), the Button can *only* be on the Stage if you want it to target a variety of Scenes. You can't put that Button within a Movie Clip on the Stage, and you can't put that Button inside of a Graphic. If you do, it loses the ability to target a Scene altogether.

It's a big bummer when you can't put a useful Button inside an interesting Movie Clip to target different Scenes. A level of interactivity is missing, which limits you. When you want to use Objects to target between random Scenes, your only functional option is a Button—on the Stage.

Graceful Hierarchies of Levels

One of the great things about Flash is creating levels. Some people compare these levels to the layers of clear, painted acetate sheets used to make cel animations, but this kind of thinking can limit you to the idea of flat art on a flat screen. A better way to think of these levels is to imagine them as panes of glass, which have some three-dimensional heft to them. And you are taking these panes of glass and putting them on top of each other in a stack.

When you look down through the plates of glass, the images on each may look like they are on one plane, but if you were to look at the stack from the side, you would see clearly that you have different image content on different levels.

Let's look at a practical application. If I were creating a web site where I have a variety of diverse content that I want to use across multiple areas, levels are the way to go. I can open up Flash, create a file that has a width of 800 and a height of 800 (800×800), and make myself a navbar (a navigation tool that will be static and appear everywhere within my Movie). When I export that Flash file, it will be known as "navbar.swf." Now let's say I want to create another static item, a copyright notice—this will be another file, 800×800 as well, with the text of my copyright notice on the bottom. I will call this "copyright.swf."

At this point I will create my master file. To do this, I'll create a new file that also has a width of 800 and a height of 800 (800×800). But I'm not going to put any images or text in here. No graphics—nothing.

Let's now look at this as if we are working with panes of glass. Each pane of glass represents a level. One level is going to hold navbar.swf; one level is going to create copyright.swf.

And now I've got my new file, the empty file. This is going to be on the pane of glass that sits on the very bottom. So it's going to be on level zero (_level0).

Now it's time to go into the basic Actions window and click Load Movie. When I click Load Movie, the dialog box pops up and asks me "What is the URL?" The answer to this is navbar.swf. Then it asks "What Location?"—in other words, it is asking, "What level do you want to put this on?"

Since this navbar will be global, I'm going to want to put it at the top of the levels I'll be deploying. Now, I personally like to use level increments of five or ten, so if I want the navbar to be on the top, I put navbar.swf on a level of 30 (though I still don't know if I want to put anything beneath it yet).

When I run the Movie, it's going to load that external.swf on the 30th level—imagine it will hover as if on a pane of glass high above the root Timeline. But if we're looking down from above and through all those panes of glass we are using, down to the Stage, it appears to be on the root Timeline—on the Stage.

Now I want to load the copyright stuff. Let's put it on Level 10.

This is a standard commercial web page, so there are going to be a couple of rather traditional sections for the navbar. One says "About the Company." The second section says "Our Portfolio." The third one says "Contact Us."

Let's open Flash, create a new file, 800×800, for the "aboutUs.swf" where I put all the graphics specific to that section and export that file. Next, I'll create a file for the "portfolio.swf" section with a lot of nice images, and I'll create some text in a file for the "contactUs.swf" section.

All right, we've got the navbar on Level 30 and the copyright on Level 10. So let's put a Button Action on Level 30 as well to load an external Movie on Level 20. Notice that this content will be underneath the navbar level but above the copyright level. When the user clicks the Button for About Us, which is on Level 30, it will load the Movie aboutUs.swf on Level 20. If they push the Button for Portfolio it will load the external Movie portfolio.swf on Level 20.

Flash will always check to see if something is already on a Level before loading a new external Movie there. When the user clicks the second button, Flash will kill the aboutUs.swf content to load portfolio.swf. If the user wants to review the About Us content again and activates that Button on Level 30, Flash will flush out portfolio.swf in order to re-load the aboutUs.swf.

It will always clear a level before it re-draws the level with its new content.

There is a good reason for putting your variable-content areas on a specific level: It is so that a Movie will load on that level in response to an action that occurs on a different level. Here we've got the navbar on Level 30. We've got the copyright on Level 10. And we have interactive content on Level 20, where action by the user (activating a Button) flushes out old content and loads the new. But notice that the user always sees the navbar and always sees the copyright information.

If I had used Scenes, I would have had to cut and paste this global material. By using levels, I just create the element once, put it on a level, and I'm good to go.

Moving Among Levels

To target content on any given level, we do not need to go down to _level0, our root Timeline. This allows for a lot more creativity even for mundane chores, such as adding a navbar and copyright notice to a web site. You don't need to know what level the user is currently on; you just need to know where the destination level is.

I can put a Movie Clip called Renee_mc inside a Movie Clip called Lockhart_mc and put this clip-within-a-clip on the copyright level, which is Level 10. I can then add a Button to activate it on the navbar, which is on Level 30.

Now my navbar level can talk to my copyright level. My direction will look something like this:

```
_level10.renee_mc.lockhart_mc.play ();
```

When the user activates the Button for the copyright, the Movie Clip Lockhart_mc will play.

This is how we use levels. It is how we target Objects on each individual pane of glass and how we can jump easily and effortlessly among levels.

You can use Load Movie to load a Movie into several places—onto several different panes of glass. Or you can load a Movie into a target that is another Movie Clip.

Sizing and Targeting

If you are loading a Movie into a level that will be used for a multi-level layered visual, every external Movie in the other levels should have the same size Stage. In the previous example, notice that all of our external Movie files were 800×800.

However, you do have to position the content with care.

The external Movies on each of the other levels—on each pane of glass—will have to be arranged in that 800×800 area so they don't overlap and get into each other's way. We don't want to obscure the navbar on our web page.

There are different ways to accomplish this. In this example, navbar.swf is going to have a lot of dead space, as will the other files, if we are loading Movies using the _level method.

A more efficient way to load external .swfs into the composition is to load a Movie into a target. I like targets a lot more than I like levels, and you'll see why.

In this method, I'm going to create the same files in different sizes. My navbar.swf will be a skinny bar that runs across the top of the web page, so it's going to have a width of 800 but a height of only 100 (800×100).

My copyright.swf is going to be even slimmer: a width of 800 and a height of 50 (800×50). To make the page look good, I'll create a "background.swf" with images and that has a width of 800 and a height of 600 (800×600). I'll then create a "content.swf" with some text in it with a width of 800 and a height of 400 (800×400).

Next, I am going to create a few Movie Clips. As in the first example, one will be a new, empty Movie Clip with a width of 800 and a height of 800 (800×800). Within this empty Movie Clip I'm going to create a few more Movie Clips that correspond to these .swf external Movie elements.

The sequence shouldn't surprise you. I'm going to create a Movie Clip and name it "Navbar," and I'm going to create and name Movie Clips called "Copyright," "Background," and another one called "Content."

But what do you think I'm going to put inside of each of these Movie Clips that I have just created and named?

Nothing. They are empty. No Graphics, no Buttons.

But let us go back to our analogy of the director on the Stage. In real theater, what happens often is that directors "block out the action" and give each actor only a certain part of the Stage to perform in. That's what we are going to do here.

When you drag an empty Movie Clip onto the Stage, it will show up as a little white circle to show that it is empty. You can use the cursor to drag these named but empty Movie Clips into the positions you want them to be in.

I am placing them at the extreme left edge of the Stage on the zero point of the x-axis:

```
x : 0
```

I will place the Navbar clip near the top of the Stage, and the Copyright clip near the bottom. I will put the Background Movie Clip slightly below the Navbar, and for a little textural interest, I will position the Content clip so it overlaps the Background area.

Now I can give the direction to my root Movie and to each Movie clip. It will look like the following:

```
_root.navbar_mc.loadMovie("navbar.swf");
```

This says, "Go to the Stage, find the empty Movie Clip named Navbar_mc, and load into the empty Movie Clip the external Movie that is navbar.swf."

In an orderly fashion I am taking navbar.swf and the other external Movies and loading them into empty Movie Clips. This is quite different from loading these different elements into separate levels, and there are going to be many advantages to it.

For one thing, I don't have to worry about lining up the elements so they will look right when all are viewed at the same time. I can just position each element quickly with a cursor. If I don't like the way they are lined up, I can just re-position them with the cursor, up or down.

For another, I am saving file size. Loading Movies into targets is a lot more flexible than loading Movies into levels.

A New Way to Make Empty Movie Clips

I've mentioned that we might want to load external .swfs into empty Movie Clips. The old way to do this was to create an empty Movie Clip in our Library, drag it onto the Stage, and position it in place, as mentioned above.

In Flash MX, it is now possible to quickly and easily create an empty Movie Clip simply by writing it out in code:

```
this.createEmptyMovieClip(instance name,depth);
```

All the program wants is for you to give the empty Movie Clip a name, and a depth, in one line of code, and then give its location in subsequent lines. Everything can be done in four lines of code.

Completed code might look like this:

```
this.createEmptyMovieClip("emptyClip_mc",1);
this.emptyClip_mc._x = 10;
this.emptyClip_mc._y = 10;
this.emptyClip_mc.loadMovie("myMovie.swf");
```

If you as an artist like to work more visually, it can still be useful to you to create an empty Movie Clip by the earlier technique so it will appear as a visible element—with the little white dot—on your screen. But if you're already pretty hard-core and find that sort of work tedious, realize that you can now create empty Movie Clips on the fly. Flash will automatically assign the empty clip an instance name so it can be called and given further directions.

Hierarchies of Movie Clips

This brings us to the question: What is the best method for hierarchy when we're talking to Movie Clips? Using **this** is like saying "do something to me"; **this** means "me." Using **_parent** means "go up one." Using **_root** means "start from the top and let's work our way down." So is the Object talking to itself? If so, then use **this**. Will it talk to other Objects? If so, decide whether you want to talk to Objects in a relative **_parent** or absolute **_root** way.

Relative addressing is not a good idea when you want Movie Clips to talk to other Movie Clips. An absolute address is more efficient. But relative addressing is helpful when you want to talk to Movie Clips that are within other Movie Clips.

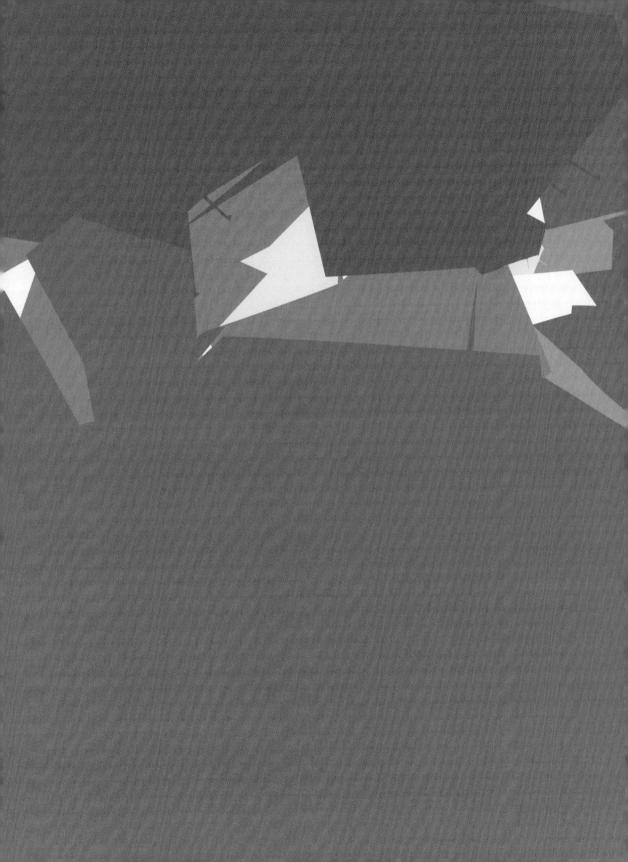

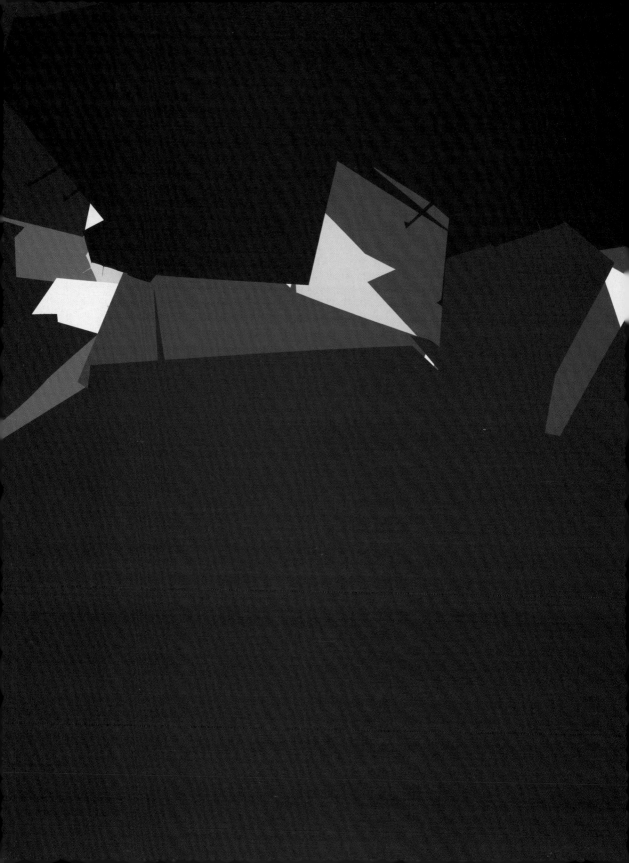

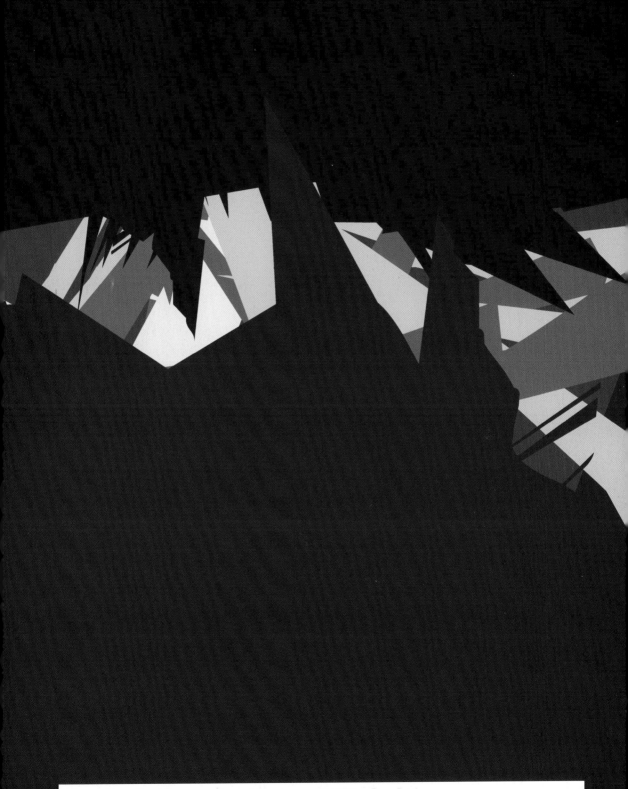

Chapter 4 - Tweening Versus ActionScript

Tweening and ActionScript are capable of doing the same things—but they do them in completely different ways.

Let's take a look at tweening first. Tweening is a frame-based animation technique. Directions in Flash to create a tween are simple: "In Frame 1, I want you, the box, to start on the left side of the Stage, and I want you to end up, at Frame 10, on the right side of the Stage." Then I can right-click with the cursor in the middle of the frames (on Macintosh the command is Ctrl+click) and call up the submenu where I will find the command, Create Motion Tween.

During playback, tweening then questions, "Where am I starting? Where I am I stopping? How many frames per second (fps) will I travel from point A to point B?" Once it has this information, the program basically figures out for itself all of the intervals and "draws" the animation of all the in-between frames. And so it creates a frame-by-frame animation of the box as it appears to move from left to right on the Stage. It will do so at a programmable rate of the specified fps. You can control the speed of the animation simply by telling it how many frames it should go along its timeline.

So that's one way to move objects.

Another way is with ActionScript. This is a scripting language, native within Flash. It is similar in some ways to JavaScript. With ActionScript, we can write code to perform that same animation function. We can give directions in code to make the box move from one side of the Stage to the other.

This raises the obvious question: Why use one technique over the other?

Well, ActionScript is obviously mathematical. The way we position an Object on the Stage and the way we will give it stage directions are by determining its original and destination locations in mathematical terms. There is nothing really difficult about this. You are just answering the questions, "Where are you on the x axis of the Stage? Where are you on the y axis of the Stage?"

So at first, the steps to move a Movie Clip seem more complicated than making a simple tween.

To understand when ActionScripting can be faster than tweening, consider the scrolling calendar found on this book's web site (**http://flashtothecore.praystation.com**). This calendar, a low gray band across the bottom of the screen, shuttles from right to left as you access the months in their usual order: January, February, March, and so on. Let's say you're visiting this site, you have looked at things in January, and you now want to look at things in December. No, wait—you want to look at June. You change your mind halfway through the process of navigating with a split second move of the cursor.

If the calendar animation had been created with tweening, there would be some problems if you were on January and then clicked December. You would have to wait for that tween to visually slide all the way, from right to left, to the end of the calendar at December. And while that is happening, the program will not accept any other input until you arrive at the destination of December.

There's no way to say, "Oh, I didn't want to go to December, I really wanted June." You have to wait until the animation completes itself. Only then will the program run the tween that shuttles the calendar bar backward from December to June.

This is awkward and time-consuming for the user, but it's even worse for me as a designer because of all the time it would take to create e*very single possibility* of moving back and forth across that calendar.

I'd have to create a tween for January to February, January to March, and so on. To make it possible for the user to access a previous month, I'd also have to make a tween from February back to January, from March back to January, and so on.

In order for a user to skip around the calendar in a free and random way, I would have to create tweens—independent animations—for *every* possible animation that would be required for a user to move from one month to another. Is the user now on June? Where is the user clicking? If the user is on June, there are 11 possible options for clicking. That would be 11 new tweens that I would have to make.

To make such a simple calendar—certainly not an unusual element for a web site—and to create what looks like a smooth movement from one month to the other, I would have to create at least 122 tweens.

And the file size would be enormous.

This is one good example of tweening not being the best choice to move things. And it's a perfect example of when to use ActionScript.

Working Offstage with ActionScript

One of the most liberating aspects of ActionScript is that it allows you to work beyond the confines of a Stage area that represents the viewable screen space—the area the audience can see. As in a real theater, there is a lot of backstage room available.

Take a good look at your main Stage again and open up the Info palette. In two-dimensional space, the Stage represents just one of four quadrants.

Locations in all of the quadrants can be described in terms of where they are located on the x axis and/or where they are located on the y axis. The center point of each axis, as noted in the Info palette, is x: 0, y: 0.

The Stage in Flash occupies only the bottom-right quarter, the space that can be described as any combination of a plus x axis (+x) and a plus y axis (+y).

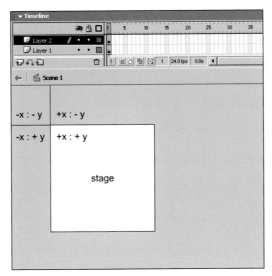

The Stage quadrant is at bottom right, corresponding to positive locations on the x and y axes.

The backstage regions are those described in the other three quadrants: the upper left "minus x, minus y" zone (–x,–y); the upper right "plus x, minus y" zone (+x,–y); and the lower left "minus x, plus y" (–x,+y) area. All of this information appears in the Info palette, in the spaces where the x and y axis numbers are recorded. If you place an Object on your screen with your cursor, the Info palette will record its location in x axis and y axis numbers.

Remember I've said that ActionScript wants to know Object locations in terms of where they can be found on the x axis and the y axis. Mathematically, these numbers can be infinite, and the placement of an Object can be anywhere in two-dimensional space. Their location just needs to be described by how far that position extends in any direction from the center axis starting point (x: 0, y: 0).

Now back to our calendar example. This time, it's going to be built with the help of ActionScript. Each month will be a width of 100, so I'm going to start with a long Movie Clip that will have a width of 1200 to accommodate them all.

I'm going to start January on the center point of the axis (x: 0, y: 0).

Now, where will February go?

It will be in the location of +100 on the x axis. March will be in the +200 location on the x axis, and so on.

To create the shuttle effect that will make the calendar slide back and forth, I'm going to create a moveable *marker* that can change its position. This marker will be able to move to the minus side of the x axis. For February, the marker will move to −100. For March, it will go to −200, and so on.

With all the positions calculated, I can begin to write an ActionScript that will allow a user to move quickly and randomly from one month to another. To allow a user to move from January to February, the ActionScript for the calendar Movie Clip needs to know only its current position on the x axis (x: 0) as it relates to the position of the marker Movie Clip, which will become its new destination (x: −100).

To allow a user to move from January to December, again all that's needed is the starting point (x: 0) and the destination (x: −1100).

And if the user decides to switch a destination—from December to June— the calendar only needs this information: "Where am I now?" "Where is my marker?" and "How much time is it going to take to get there?"

If, at the split second the decision is made, the action has reached x: −423, the program will mathematically identify this current location. To reach the new location, it will do its mathematical equation along the x axis and calculate the difference between those two points. Once it has calculated the difference, it can execute a move to the desired destination, x: −600.

The math is pretty easy, just a few lines of code. We need only the following information:

1. The current location of the marker Movie Clip on the x axis.

2. The current location of the calendar Movie Clip on the x axis.

3. The difference between the location of the marker Movie Clip and the calendar Movie Clip.

4. The speed of the movement across the distance.

5. The command to execute the calculation and do the move.

The following code, then, allows a movement from January to June, or any month to any other month:

```
marker = _root.marker_mc._x;
calendar = _root.calendar_mc._x;
difference = marker-calendar;
speed = difference/2;
_root.calendar_mc._x = calendar_mc + speed;
```

So here's a case where you could either spend your time writing 122 different tweens—or write five lines of code.

Mixing It Up

I like mixing ActionScripts and tweening. Chapter 8, "The Perfect Fade," shows how to use ActionScripts and tweens to move forward and backward in a Timeline. With this very simple use of ActionScripting and tweening working together, we can create some pretty interesting visuals.

Among Flash designers, I meet a lot of people who are purely into tweening; I also meet a lot of people who use only ActionScript. Why not mix the two? You can produce interactive yet cinematic effects.

Chapter 5 - Everything Else About Movie Clips

For me, the most important thing to think about when starting to create a Movie Clip is, well, actually a couple of things:

- The fact that you can name Movie Clips, which means they can be talked to and given directions when you write ActionScript.
- The fact that Movie Clips can have their own Timelines, independent of the root Timeline.

Among the assets of Flash, Movie Clips can do a lot of things that other elements cannot do. To properly get your head around the ways to make Movie Clips do what you want, you have to understand their unique capabilities and add to your foundation by exploring the quirks and accidents of their potential.

Name Movie Clips Consistently

I've mentioned that I'm a maniac for using the Library and its folders to organize projects as well as the importance of naming the Objects in your Library in the most simple and accessible way. Well, it pays to consistently name each of your Objects, especially at that point when you drag them out of the Library onto the Stage—the point where, in Flash terminology, they become *instances*.

The ability to name Movie Clips is important because it means they can be called by their names and given directions for their actions on the Stage. Naming in a thoughtful way simply helps you keep track of Movie Clips just a little bit better. And it is the one of the best ways to keep track of your work when you are doing a lot of projects.

My own method is very simple. I've mentioned how I name Movie Clips in my Library folders:

```
01 - director
02 - actor Oliver Mycat
03 - actor Ashley Mycat
```

When I pull a Movie Clip onto my Stage, I give it an instance name that is similar to its Library Folder name. So if I have named a Movie Clip "01 - actor Oliver Mycat," when I pull it onto my Stage, I might name the instance "oliverMycat_mc."

Notice that I've altered the name only slightly for the instance, using lowercase for the first letter of the first name and a capital letter only on the last name.

This appears similar but is dissimilar in a very consistent way. It is another simple discipline to speed up changes as you work, when you're moving back and forth between the working environments of the Stage and the Library.

This is something that's going to save you when it's 3:00 a.m. and you're really tired and the project is due tomorrow morning.

Also remember that Flash MX gives the functionality of Buttons to Movie Clips and some functions of Movie Clips to Buttons. If you're going to be using a Button like a Movie Clip, you may want to add "_mc" to your Button's name and its instance name.

Put a Stop Before You Go

As mentioned earlier, one of the beautiful things about the Movie Clip is that it has its own independent Timeline. Let's say I am going to place a Movie Clip on the Stage, but I don't want the playhead to just start running it. To do this, I will put a stop command in the first frame of that Movie Clip's own Timeline. Now, when the playhead reaches that Movie Clip, it will stop on the first frame.

Why would I do this? It's because, as the playhead is moving across the root Timeline, I may be introducing Movie Clips over a period of time.

Let's go back to the example of that standard commercial web page built in Chapter 3, "Hierarchies and Object Relations." I may not want all the elements, which I created as Movie Clips, to appear on the screen all at once. Maybe I want the Navbar Movie Clip to appear first, then the copyright will fade in, then the background, then the content.

Remember that Flash has to be told *everything*. When that playhead hits that Movie Clip, the first thing it's going to do is try to play that Movie Clip. It says, "Oh, I've reached a Movie Clip that has its own independent Timeline. Let's go."

But my first frame tells it, "No, no, no—let's stop."

So the minute the playhead hits the Movie Clip that I introduced on the root Timeline, the first thing it is going to do is stop on that Movie Clip's very first frame. I've told it to stop there.

Here's a good analogy: Once again, I'm not the director; I'm the nursery school teacher. All of my kids don't show up at the school all at once. The parents bring the children at certain times, over a period of time as the school day begins. First Child1A_mc comes, then Child2A_mc comes, then Child3A_mc comes, and so on.

As the teacher, I have to settle them all down first. "Okay, be quiet," the teacher says. "Sit down and be quiet. Be quiet." As they come in, the teacher is settling them down.

Once all the kids have arrived, the teacher can finally say, "Welcome to class," and class can begin. I can call the children by name and give them things to do. I can give them questions to respond to.

Let's say I point to the Movie Clip named Child1A_mc first and say:

"Child1A_mc, what's two plus two?" All the other children are quiet.

Child1A_mc says, "Four."

Now I tell Child1A_mc to be quiet again so I can speak to another Movie Clip.

This time I will say, "Child2A_mc, what's your current position in this space?"

"I'm at x: 100, y: 100," replies Child2A_mc.

To get the children to answer questions in order, the teacher has to settle them all down first. It's the same thing with Movie Clips. As that playhead is moving, the first thing the director should tell the Movie Clips is: "Stop. Be quiet. Don't do anything until I direct you or until I give you a question to answer."

Every time we add a stop point in a Movie Clip's first frame, we give ourselves a fresh opportunity to build in some user interactivity. Take this opportunity whenever it makes sense—and, creatively, even when it does not. Flash movies can reach far, far beyond the linear limitations of film or video. We don't have to content ourselves with Play, Fast-Forward, Reverse, or Stop, like we do on a VCR. The interactive experience with the audience can bring real drama to the Theater of the web. There's a lot of ground to cover and a lot that can be discovered before we need to decide whether or not Bob should die. (See Chapter 1, "Introduction: Mentalities and Anomalies.")

Remember that life gets easier when the teacher doesn't have too many students in the first place. You don't want *too* many things happening on your Stage at any one time because the computer will have to think about too much. The more Movie Clips you use, the more work Flash has to manage with its resources and processing.

Align to the Axis Zero Points

We've talked about putting Objects into Objects on your Stage, such as putting little boxes inside bigger boxes. Here is a method to help you keep better track of those Objects once you've put one Object into another and so can't see them clearly anymore.

Whenever you open up a Movie Clip, you'll see a set of crosshairs that appears in the middle. The center of those crosshairs indicates the center point of that Movie Clip in its own two-dimensional space: It is 0 on the x axis and 0 on the y axis. As with the Stage, this set of crosshairs is dividing the two-dimensional area of that Movie Clip into four quadrants: upper left, upper right, lower left, and lower right.

When I bring a new Movie Clip (or any other Object) into another Movie Clip, I prefer to align that new Movie Clip or Object to the lower-right quadrant of the center axis of the Stage. I will place it at that center point, which is x: 0, y: 0. On the screen it's going to look like the embedded Object is "hanging" off those lower corners and extending into the lower right. If I refer to the Info palette, I can confirm that my location values for the embedded Object are x: 0, y: 0.

There is a good reason for parking Movie Clips within Movie Clips on the x: 0, y: 0 point. If you are going to use these Movie Clips in conjunction with ActionScript, you want to be able to describe their location in two-dimensional space (_x and _y) quickly in mathematical terms. If you want to move other Objects around within a Movie Clip, you are going to want to know their positions as well. ActionScript will specifically want to know what their (_x) position is and/or what their (_y) position is.

If I've made a practice of aligning these Objects to the axis position of x: 0, y: 0, I automatically know the starting location of those Objects, even if they've been embedded within a Movie Clip. I don't have to bother looking at the Info palette to see what their two-dimensional location is. I know the location of the external Movie Clip is x: 0, y: 0 on my Stage, and know that the internal Object is parked on x: 0, y: 0 within the Movie Clip.

Then, if I want to write ActionScript that causes the Object to move to another location on the Stage—for example if I then want the Object to move to x: 100 on the x axis, or if I want to give directions to move a Movie Clip that's been embedded into another Movie Clip, I can program both the start point and the end point very quickly and precisely. I know that it is mathematically perfect: It's in proportion. This precise alignment is extremely valuable.

Let's look at our Stage with this new understanding. We know the upper-left corner of the visible screen is x: 0, y: 0. We will plan to place a Movie Clip in that upper-left corner. We know that within the crosshairs of that Movie Clip we can hang another embedded Object at the lower-right quadrant of its crosshairs, at the Movie Clip's own center point of 0,0.

Now we want that embedded Movie Clip to move to the x position of zero (x: 0) on the Stage. We know that both the horizontal edge and the vertical edge of the first Movie Clip are going to line up where we want them to. But if my crosshair is at one place and my embedded Movie Clip is at another more arbitrary point on the x axis, that embedded Object is not going to be truly aligned on the Stage. It's going to be off just that little bit. It won't know to do the x: 0 of the edge; it will just do the x: 0 of the crosshairs.

The crosshair has to be the same so it can be flush.

In the case of Chapter 4's calendar example, which slides back and forth in response to user input, there's no question that −100 is going to slide exactly to February, −200 is going to slide exactly to the start of March, and so on. There isn't going to be any sloppiness: The user isn't going to be presented with a calendar where all the Sundays of the month seem to have fallen off and are missing.

So, align your Movie Clips and the Objects within them to an axis point that is x: 0, y: 0. This will give you a certain precision alignment in your projects and do quite a bit to speed the rest of the work along.

Chapter 6 - Introduction to Flash MX

I know what you're thinking at this point: "Okay, enough with the philosophy; I just want to learn ActionScript!" You may actually have been tempted to skip all the previous chapters and try to start writing code.

Well, there are a million ways to work in Flash. I can teach you my way; someone else will teach you their way. But if you don't have a philosophy to back you up and a passion to play, to experiment, to see things differently, and to find beauty in confusion, then none of this will ever help you.

So, even if you feel you already know how to program Flash, or have worked in Flash 4 or 5, let me begin by saying this: Some things are different in Flash MX.

As I've noted, panels and palettes are different in Flash MX; the Property Inspector combines several into one. The capabilities of Buttons and Movie Clips are different, and, in many cases, they can be interchangeable.

Coding Changes

In Flash 5 we had our code all over the place; it is now more efficient to write most code in just one place. Macromedia suggests that you do it on the root Timeline. What I've been doing to keep this a bit more organized is to create a new layer on my root Timeline and name it "actions." I then write all the code for my actions—all the code that affects the entire movie—in this one layer.

Another significant change in writing code is that Clip Events have morphed into Event Methods, and these can also be written into the code in the root Timeline. Previously, we had to attach event-related code to a Movie Clip in the Object Actions window when specifying the event (onLoad, onEnterFrame, and so on) that would trigger an action.

We don't have to do this anymore. Instead, we can simply create a Movie Clip (myMovieClip_mc) and write the code in the root Timeline as follows:

```
myMovieClip_mc.onEnterFrame
```

Some other enhancements make it much easier to work in Flash MX. For example, the Object Actions window now sports line numbers along the side when you're writing code, and allows you to set breakpoints. Line numbers and breakpoints are very helpful when you're doing a line-by-line debugging of a program.

Listeners

Another innovation are the *listeners*. A listener notifies the program when an action has been taken—for example, when the user's mouse or keyboard key has been pressed and activated. You create a listener for a specific Object, and then define a function that will occur when the mouse is pressed. You can create listeners for mouse actions, such as onMouseDown, onMouseMove, and onMouseUp. You can also create listeners for keyboard actions, such as onKeyUp or onKeyDown.

> Note: For more details, you can look up listeners in the Flash MX Reference palette, which contains reference descriptions for ActionScript. Go to the Window menu in the top tool bar, open up the Reference menu, and scroll down to the following sub-menus: Object, Movie, then Mouse. There you'll find Listeners.

If you've added a listener to a Movie for an onMouseDown, for example, when the user presses the mouse, the listener says, "Yo! We've got a MouseDown!" and notifies or wakes up the rest of the program to run functions and execute actions.

This can make an entire program more efficient. Previously, clip events such as onEnterFrame ran continuously within your program, remaining constantly poised to execute a command on demand. This code would be constantly running, even if a user never applied a mouse or a keystroke event. By contrast, listeners wait off the side, preserving processing until an action actually occurs.

What's even more interesting is that multiple listeners can be set up to receive notification of a single user event.

Here's a sample you'll find on the book's web site that you can try yourself:

```
ears = new Object();
ears.onMouseDown = function() {
    trace("mousedown");
};
ears.onKeyDown= function() {
    trace("keydown");
}
Key.addListener(ears);
Mouse.addListener(ears);
```

I've only used trace so there is no art, but I have created two listeners that will respond to a user's actions. One is a response to a press of the mouse (onMouseDown) and the other responds to a key press (onKeyDown).

If you run this movie, when you press either the mouse or a key, the output window on your screen will simply notify you that you've pressed the mouse button or a key.

The implications, of course, are much broader. The function you design can be a very complicated set of code that triggers several complex events, but that part of the program will only run when the listener notifies or "wakes up" that function.

The Basic Tutorials

The basic tutorials in the following five chapters were designed to provide you with a strong base in syntax and logic for writing ActionScript. They will strengthen your understanding of the philosophy behind ActionScript. You will learn how elements, such as Movie Clips, can be used not just as screen elements, but also as drivers for increasingly complex and highly interactive projects.

These tutorials are based on simple ideas that involve, individually, at most four or five lines of code. You'll learn how to isolate the code to make it generic, modular, and reusable, so it can become part of your foundation. Soon, you'll be writing code so fast that you'll never use a drop-down menu ever again.

If you're already hard-core with ActionScript, you might want to skip ahead to Chapter 13, "Friction," for the intermediate and advanced tutorials. But you might miss a lot. The basic projects include some shortcuts I use every day in my own work. They may help you speed your way through your own art and client work, and may even open up some avenues of creativity that you haven't thought of.

Part II - Projects: Basic Projects

Chapter 7 - Movie Clips as Buttons and the One Button Trick

One of the biggest changes in Flash MX is that Movie Clips can be given many of the capabilities of Buttons. In earlier versions, codes that referenced a user's mouse actions—onRollover, onPress, onRelease, and onReleaseOutside—had to be applied or attached to a Button.

Because Movie Clips now can act like Buttons, we can write something like this:

```
MyMovieClip._mc.onPress
```

This triggers an onPress event when someone presses a mouse over the specified Movie Clip. In most cases, there is no need for a Button interface between the user and the Movie Clip.

Just because the technique is new, however, doesn't mean using Movie Clips as Buttons is always the best way to create a user interface. The technique for the One Button Trick extends the functionality of a Button in a slightly different way, as the following project demonstrates.

Exploring Button States

Let's begin by reviewing how Buttons work in Flash. Start by making a rectangular box:

1. Using the Rectangle tool and the Arrow tool, draw a new rectangle on the Stage. Make it 20×20. Use the Arrow tool to select it, and press F8 to turn this Object into a Button. Name it "00 - trans" (for "transparent Button"). Check to see if it is in your Library.

2. Using the Align tool, align the left corner of the rectangle to 0 on the x axis and 0 on the y axis. Check the numbers in your Info palette to make sure the x, y coordinates are correct before moving on. (You know how crazy I am about aligning things.)

There are four possible ways to work Buttons. In Flash they are called *states*:

- Up
- Over
- Down
- Hit

3. To experience all the states, double-click on your Button to open it and see the Timeline. At this point, the vector appears in only the first key frame, Frame 1, and the default state of the Button is Up.

4. Select key frame 2 and press F6 to duplicate the box into Frame 2. Press F6 again and again, and place duplicates of the vector in Frame 3 and in Frame 4.

This simple procedure reveals the other three states: Over, Down, and Hit. There is one in each of the four key frames, and each frame now contains a copy of the box.

The first three states are self-explanatory. If the cursor has not been placed directly on the vector, that's the Up state. If the cursor merely rolls over the vector, that's Over. If the cursor is directly on the vector and mouse pressure is applied, that's Down. The Hit state designates any hot spot that activates the Button to prompt an action. But the Hit state, located in Frame 4, is far more flexible: The position of the hot spot does not have to correspond to the visual image of the vector. It doesn't have to be the same size or even be in the same part of the screen.

The hot spot area of the Hit state is defined by the shape of the vector that you put in that frame. This shape is transparent; it is invisible on the screen. This solved one of the biggest Button problems that Flash had in the past.

Many designers like to use text as a Button—for example, the typed words "HELLO WORLD." When a user clicks on the words HELLO WORLD, a responsive action then occurs.

The problem was that the user had to click on the solid body of a letter. If the user's cursor happened to be in the "empty" space in the middle of the "O" in HELLO, nothing would register and nothing would happen.

The Hit state solves this problem. It defines the area of screen space for the hot spot, and embraces all within it.

5. Delete the vectors in Up (Frame 1), Over (Frame 2), and Down (Frame 3). Leave that last 20×20 vector in Frame 4, in the Hit state.

Look at your Stage. Whatever color your rectangle was originally, it should now be a shade of teal blue, and it should be 50 percent transparent. That's Flash letting you know that the vectors in the Button you created are residing in the Hit state only.

6. This next step will help you get familiar with how to redefine the hot spot area. Because our original size for the vector was only 20×20 and we want this Button to be generic, we want to be able to resize it to fit any sort of hot spot. To do this, simply go into the Info palette and resize the button to 100×20. You might even make it 100×100 or 200×200.

As we move on to the rest of the interface, the point to remember is that the hot spot is scalable, because it is invisible.

Creating the User Interface

Having defined the hot spot area, let's identify it for the user.

7. Still working in the same file, use the Type tool and type your name on the Stage.

8. At this point, use the Arrow keys to place the transparent Button, which should already be on the Stage, on top of your name.

   Note: Sizing the transparent Button assumes that 100×20, or whatever size you selected, is a large enough area to fit over the name. If your name is longer, take a moment to go back into the Info palette and resize the Button so it fits.

9. Using the Arrow tool, drag and select both the Button and the text you just typed, and press the F8 key. Select Movie Clip for the type of Object, and name it "01 - myName."

In your Library you should now have two elements:

> 00 - trans
> 01 - myName

The transparent Button is now inside of the Movie Clip (Objects within Objects).

A Simple Animation Sequence

There's no point in having a Button that doesn't prompt an action. For the sake of this tutorial, we'll do a very simple frame jump: When the user does certain mouse moves and approaches the text of your name, your name will change color.

10. Double-click on the Movie Clip 01 - myName and view its Timeline. Now, add two layers. Give the lower layer the title "name," the middle layer "button," and the upper layer "actions."

11. Right now, everything is on the name layer, so the next step is to move the transparent Button into the button layer. To do this, select the Button, then press Ctrl+X to cut. Highlight the second layer, and press Ctrl+Shift+V, which is the shortcut for Paste in Place. (You can also use the Distribute to Layers shortcut: Ctrl+Shift+D.)

12. Select the name layer, and press F6 to add key frames and duplicate the text of your name into the next frame. Pressing once duplicates the text into Frame 2; pressing F6 again duplicates it into Frame 3.

13. Color your text. For this tutorial, select the text in Frame 1 and make it blue. In Frame 2, make the text color a lighter blue. In Frame 3, make the text red.

14. Now you need your transparent Button to span all three frames. To do this, move your cursor on to Frame 3 of the button layer in the Timeline. Press F5 to "open up" the Button to span across Frames 1, 2, and 3.

15. In the actions layer of this Timeline, use the Object Actions menu to put a stop command in each of the three frames:

    ```
    stop();
    ```

Technically, you need to put a stop in the first frame only. I've gotten in the habit of putting in multiple stops, however, largely because I'm paranoid about control. In your future projects, the choice is entirely up to you.

Writing the Button Code

The final phase of this project is to add the code to your button.

16. Select the Button 00 - trans, and go into the Object Actions window. If you are in Flash's default mode, which is Normal mode, you should see a hierarchical menu on the left side.

Select Object, Movie, Button, Events, and you'll see a deeper sub-menu that describes all the things a user's mouse might do: press, release, releaseOutside, keyPress, rollOver, rollOut, dragOver, and dragOut.

For this tutorial, we'll select rollover as the mouse event, but we're not going to select it from the submenu. We are going to start writing ActionScript. From this point on, we will be working entirely in Expert mode, and we won't be using Normal mode for the rest of the book.

17. Switch to Expert mode. In the Object Actions window, write this code:

```
on (release, rollOver) {
    this.gotoAndStop(2);
}
on (rollOut, dragOut) {
    this.gotoAndStop(1);
}
on (press) {
    this.gotoAndStop(3);
}
```

You have just written directions for *five different* mouse events the user may attempt. When the user rolls the cursor over the transparent Button, the Movie Clip will go to and stop on its second frame. If the user continues to roll the cursor off the hot spot or drags the cursor away from that area, the Movie Clip will go to and stop on its first frame. If the user gets excited by the change in color and decides to press down upon the mouse, the Movie Clip will go to and stop on the third frame, which turns the text red.

What's the Point?

I know what you're thinking. We could have just made a regular Button that the user could press. Why go the long way and make a transparent Button? Why go to all the bother of making a Movie Clip and actually having to write lines of code?

Well, a regular Button can handle only three states: Up, Over, and Down. With this technique, I've used a single, transparent Button to control the calendar at the *Praystation* web site and accommodate *nine* states that correspond to user actions. This program (which can be visited at **http:// flashtothecore.praystation.com**) tracks which calendar dates the web site visitor has not yet clicked on (Up, Over, and Down), where the visitor is currently (Up, Over, and Down), and what the visitor clicked on and viewed previously (Up, Over, and Down) with nine colors.

Instead of having six Buttons on your screen that have a bunch of different functions, why not have just one button that addresses all the variations of what a Button can do? The user presses down with the mouse and something happens. The user rolls over a hot spot, absentmindedly, and something else happens.

The One Button Trick assumes a certain intelligence on the part of the user. While mousing around the screen, the user quickly learns where the hot spots are. I know artists who have built web sites with Flash and put a few transparent Buttons for hot spots that are invisible to the viewer. An inadvertent move of the mouse, for example, suddenly triggers an event.

I would attribute 100 percent of my success in this industry to simply being willing to go the extra mile. Everything you put on a screen should add value—not just take up screen space.

Chapter 8 - The Perfect Fade

This project should be helpful to animators: It will show you how to use ActionScript to control tweening and create a softer, more elegant fading effect than the average tween.

If you've looked at the example on the book's web site, you know this will be a very simple animation: Some lines of cross marks fade up and down, appearing and reappearing when the user activates a button on the screen. Using ActionScript with tweening, you will be able to create a smooth, gliding motion to your fade effects, so they won't suffer from jitter. You can use this technique to create smooth transitions for all sorts of animations.

In fact, one of the motivations for this was to help out some friends of mine over at **www.jibjab.com** who had a cartoon that was giving them trouble. When the user moused onto on an image of a closed box, a little character was supposed to pop up. Whenever the user would mouse off the box, however, the little character would vanish. Flash would simply return to the first frame of the tween, which of course showed only a closed box. Instead, the animators wanted the character to retract itself back into the box. When the user moused on or off the box, they wanted the character to go up and down, like a jack-in-the-box, in a flexible, accordion-like motion. The solution we devised was an animation technique that could interact more rapidly and smoothly with a user's mouse movements, moving forward and backward in a realistic way.

Creating the Tween

To try this technique, the first thing you need is an Object to fade, so make some art. For the online tutorial, I created a bunch of random vectors—a series of crosshairs that fade up. I suggest that you create a simple rectangle.

1. Use the Arrow tool to select the shape you just made, and press the F8 key to turn the Object into a Movie Clip. Name it "02 - fadeBox."

2. Because the Object is going to fade, we'll want to control its Alpha (transparency) level. But we can't adjust Alpha on vectors—it has to be another Object. So go into 02 - fadeBox and select the vectors again. Press F8, but turn this new Object into a Graphic this time. Name it "01 - fadeBox Art."

3. Now that you have turned your vectors into a Graphic Object, you can create a tween. Open up the Movie Clip 02 - fadeBox. In its Timeline, click on Frame 20, then press F6 to create a key frame on Frame 20 and duplicate the Graphic.

4. Right-click anywhere between Frames 1 and 20 on the Timeline, and choose Create Motion Tween. This simple command creates a motion tween that goes from Frame 1 to Frame 20.

5. To create the fade effect, select Frame 1 on the Timeline, then select that Graphic Symbol. There is no Effects palette in Flash MX. Instead, when you select the Graphic Symbol, the Property Inspector offers you a menu of options for graphics. In the drop-down menu box for Color, select Alpha. Set the Alpha level (level of transparency of the Graphic) to 0 for Frame 1 only.

Controlling the Alpha level is the key to the perfect fade, as you'll soon see.

Solving Jitter and Jags

Jitter and jags are a common problem in Flash when you are working with images, JPEGs, GIFs, and PNGs. It happens whenever the image enters and then exits an Alpha state. You may have noticed this problem in your own work, as animations and images seem to "shift pixels" in a jagged, ragged way in your movies. This always happens when the program has to suddenly shift from a state of Alpha to its default state of None.

The solution to the problem, however, is pretty simple. We're not going to let the Alpha levels *ever* get to None.

A simple procedure lets you trick the program:

6. Go back to your work in progress, the fading box tween, and select Frame 20. Select the Graphic Symbol, go into the Color menu on the Property Inspector, and choose Alpha, so you can make a little adjustment.

7. Highlight the Percentage field, and type in a maximum Alpha level of 99%. Your tween now fades up smoothly and gracefully, because it is running happily through frames with Alpha levels of 0, 1, 2, 3, 20, 50, 60, 90, 97, 98, and 99%. The tween never experiences the None state, because it never reaches the Alpha level of 100%.

Take this advice whenever you are creating a fade up effect and want to avoid that irritating jump or glitch. Never use an Alpha level of None or its equivalent, 100%. Instead, adjust it down, at least one notch, to 99%.

8. As a finishing touch to the 02 - fadeBox Movie Clip, open its Timeline, create a new layer, and name the layer "actions." Put a stop command in this layer's first frame:

   stop();

Now, let's move on.

Designing the User Interface
for the Fade

The user will activate the animation with an invisible button. Go ahead and create one now. If you need help, look over the steps for the One Button Trick in Chapter 7. In the web site example for this project, I put a transparent Button over a bit of text that says "Touch Me."

9. After you've created your own transparent Button and its text, highlight the Button and give it an instance name of "trans_mc."

We will evaluate the user's mouse actions as they occur using the code we attach to the Button. The mouse events we'll use are rollover and rollout/dragOut.

Because we simply want to see if the user is rolling the cursor over the target area (hot spot) or not, we can do this evaluation as a simple yes-or-no, true-or-false proposition. If the cursor has rolled over the hot spot, that will equal true. If the cursor has not rolled on or has rolled off, that will equal false.

10. Select the Button, and open its Object Actions window.

11. Now, write this code in Expert mode:

```
on (rollover){
    _root.fade = true;
}
```

This sets a variable on the root Timeline equal to the value of true. When you've written this yourself, you'll notice the word "true" turns blue. That's the indication that true is a reserved word for Boolean values. (In mathematics, a Boolean value is a true or false statement.)

12. Write the next statements:

```
on (rollout,dragOut){
    _root.fade = false;
}
```

Note that in addition to rollout, I've included the mouse movement dragOut. That's just in case somebody clicks on the phrase "Touch Me" and drags the cursor away. You'll notice how false also turns blue when you type the second line, an indication that this is also a reserved word for a Boolean value.

You now have a user interface. Something will happen when the user moves the cursor on top of the Touch Me button, and something will happen when the cursor moves off of the Touch Me hot spot.

Fade Up Meets Fade Down

Next, we will write the code on the root Timeline that will allow the box to fade up and down in response to the touch of the Button. We've already used tweening to make the box fade up smoothly, from transparent to opaque. The second part of the animation, getting the box to "fade down" or disappear from the screen, is handled with ActionScript. Remember, Flash can move forward in time only, so to make an animation move "in reverse" is a bit tricky. Even so, all it takes is a few lines of code.

13. Write this on the root Timeline:

```
fscommand ("fullscreen", "false");
fscommand ("allowscale", "false");
stop();

// don't use the hand icon
trans_mc.useHandCursor = false;

// handle the onEnterFrame event
fadeBox_mc.onEnterFrame = function() {
    if (fade) {
        this.nextFrame();
    } else {
        this.prevFrame();
    }
};
```

The first two lines should look familiar. We're putting a stop in the first frame and making the little hand cursor icon invisible on the screen.

The third line sets up the event method (what used to be called a Clip Event). Because we're using onEnterFrame, the next action will be repeated in a continuous loop. This repeated action is described as a *function*, and the last few lines of the code describe what that function will be.

The job of this function will be to evaluate and respond to the true and false aspects of the user's mouse movements. This is done in the form of an if/else statement. Essentially, the program will evaluate if something is true—in this case, whether or not the cursor is on top of the transparent Button's hot spot. If it's not—if it's false—the program will turn to the else part of the statement.

If/Else Statements

The program will now look to see if the user's cursor is on the Button's hot spot. In other words, it will ask: "Hey, am I on this? Does fade equal true?" (That is, it checks if _root.fade equals true.) If the answer back is "Yes, fade is equal to true," the program says, "Great! Now I know what to do. I must move forward one frame—to my next frame."

Because you chose onEnterFrame as the event method, this sequence will run as a continuous loop. The program will continue to advance the tween, one frame at a time (Frame 1, 2, 3, 4, 5, 6, 7, 8, 9, 10, and so on up to 20). But—and this is important—it will continue to advance frame by frame *only as long as the user stays on the Button.*

As soon as the user moves off, then _root.fade equals false and the program moves on to the else part of the statement. And it knows what to do: "I go back one frame to my previous frame." Now the tween goes backwards. If the user mouses off by the time the tween had reached Frame 10, the program moves to Frame 9, 8, 7, 6, 5, 4, 3, 2, and 1.

Now you can understand why this is called the "perfect" fade. While the tween will begin on its Frame 1 the first time the button is activated, it will not fade up all the way to Frame 20 if the user decides to mouse off. Instead, the tween begins to fade down just as soon as the button is de-activated. The fade will continue up and down in a smooth motion as long as the user moves the mouse on or off the hot spot. The if/else coding attached to the Movie Clip and the true-false coding attached to the Button constantly evaluate the mouse movements and give the appropriate directions to the tween.

You can of course do more than fading with this technique. What you've really learned is how to use ActionScript to control tweening—any kind of tweening. This technique can also be used on the independent Timelines of Movie Clips, allowing you or a user to "rock" a Movie Clip sequence forward and backward in time.

Chapter 9 - Collision Detection: Drag and Drop

Drag and Drop is more than simply dragging an object across the screen with a cursor, then dropping it onto a target point. More generally this is a method for collision detection. On screen, once two Objects have crossed paths, that moment can be noticed or detected and become a trigger point to set off actions and reactions that move a story along.

The classic application is the online "shopping cart." In real life, when you go to a supermarket, you wheel a shopping cart down the aisles, taking objects off the shelves and dropping them into the basket of your cart. Online, the basket is a *hot spot* on the screen. When a user drags an object across the screen to the hot spot, the program detects this intersection and executes further commands.

Collision detection is also important in gaming. If you are a game developer creating a rocket ship that shoots bullets at enemy ships, the game program needs to know when the bullet collides with the enemy ship, to trigger the animation for blowing it up on screen. A collision detection program can be far more detailed with many defined variables that detect how and where the collision between the bullet and the ship occurs. These can in turn trigger a variety of outcomes: from a ding on the hull of the enemy ship to a direct hit that blows up the enemy with spectacular special effects.

Finding and Using Hit Test

The method used for collision detection in Flash MX is Hit Test, which replaced the earlier DropTarget method. Hit Test is a bit buried in the drop-down menus. To find it, open the Objects menu, then open the sub-menus Movie, Movie Clip, and Method.

Hit Test is more sophisticated than DropTarget. It automatically evaluates the instance supplied by any Movie Clip to see if it overlaps or intersects with a designated *hit area*. The hit area is a hot spot that you identify using a Movie Clip's name or a set of x,y coordinates.

The hit area can have a boundary that is defined by x and y coordinates and that is invisible on the screen. This means that an Object doesn't have to actually collide visually with the other Object to record the drop or hit; it simply has to encounter the hit area.

With Hit Test, the user does not have to let go of the Object by releasing pressure on the mouse to record a hit or collision. As long as the user keeps dragging the Object around the screen, Hit Test will continue to evaluate its relative location to the hot spot, reporting back whenever the Object has collided, overlapped, rolled over, or otherwise intersected with that other Object.

Create Two Objects to Collide

To help you get your head around this properly, you'll need to have two Objects that can collide. So, open up Flash, and create two Movie Clips.

1. Use the Rectangle tool to create a dark gray box. This will be the target, the hot spot, for the moving Object. Name this Movie Clip "01 - dropTarget." This element on your Stage is not going to move, so you don't have to do anything else to it. Drag it onto your Stage and give it the instance name of "dropTarget_mc."

2. The second Movie Clip to make should be a slightly smaller rectangle. This is the Object that gets dragged around and dropped. Create it as 02 - drag in your Library, then drag it to your Stage and give it the instance name of "drag_mc."

You should now have on your Stage two Objects with two separate names.

Set Up the User Interface

We want to give the user a confirmation when the drag-and-drop action is completed successfully. So, open up the 02 - drag_mc Movie Clip.

3. Name the bottom layer of its Timeline "vectors."

4. Highlight Frame 2 in the vectors layer, and press F6 to make a copy of the vector.

5. In Frame 1, make the rectangle a medium shade of gray.

6. In Frame 2, make the rectangle a lighter shade of gray.

7. Add a new layer to this Movie Clip's Timeline, and name it "Stops." Put this above the vector layer. Put a **stop();** command in Frame 1, and another **stop();** command in Frame 2.

In Step 7, you are adding an extra bit of user interactivity. Later, when you write the code, you will ask this Movie Clip to jump to its second frame when the user releases the mouse while it is sitting on top of the target Object. When the Movie Clip jumps, it will change the color and turn the box from medium gray to light gray. This will let the user know that an action has been successfully performed.

Writing the Code for the onPress

One of the great things about Flash MX is that we don't need Buttons to the same extent as we did in the past. Because Movie Clips can act as Buttons, we can give the directions for any mouse event to a Movie Clip. So directions we might have given to a Button in Flash 5, such as onPress or onRelease, can be written in MX on the root Timeline to directly affect a Movie Clip, without the need for a Button intermediary between the user and the Object.

8. Create a new layer on the root Timeline. Name this layer "actions" and write the following code:

```
fscommand ("fullscreen", "false");
fscommand ("allowscale", "false");
stop();

// don't use the hand icon
drag_mc.useHandCursor = false;

// handle press event
drag_mc.onPress = function() {
    this.startDrag(false, 26, 25, 613, 170);
    this.onMouseMove = function() {
        updateAfterEvent();

    };
```

Notice we've also made the hand cursor icon invisible once again. After that, when the user moves the cursor to the gray box, and presses down on the mouse, the function kicks in and the drag action will begin.

In the subsequent statement, **this** specifies what is being dragged. In this case, the rectangle is dragging itself. If you were planning to drag some other object, you could change **this** to the name of a different instance.

The first parameter can be the words "true" or "false," and it refers to an Attribute of whether you want to lock mouse to the center. We do not want the object to lock to the center of the cursor, so we've put false.

The rest of the information concerns an Attribute called Constrain to Rectangle. You often want to confine the movements of an Object to certain spaces on your screen, particularly if a user is going to be dragging that Object around. In the case of this tutorial, the Object can be dragged only to the limits of the visible area of the Stage.

When you select Constrain to Rectangle in Normal mode, four empty input fields appear, each indicating the Left (L), Right (R), Top (T), and Bottom (B) of the screen space, as defined by x and y coordinates. You simply fill in the coordinates to define the space, and these numbers will appear automatically in the second line.

In the online tutorial, the coordinates are 26, 25, 613, and 170, and can be seen in the input boxes and in the line of code.

The last two lines of code are a direction for something that will happen every time the user moves the mouse. When there is an onMouseMove event, a function, updateAfterEvent, will be executed.

The updateAfterEvent line is necessary to make the action independent of the frame rate for the movie. This eliminates any lag time between the movement of the user's mouse and the corresponding movement of the small rectangle. Both are small enhancements so the program's response to a user can be smoother and more transparent.

9. Write the next bit of code right after the first, to describe the function that will be executed when the user releases pressure on the mouse:

```
// handle release event
drag_mc.onRelease = drag_mc.onReleaseOutside = function() {
    stopDrag();
    this.onMouseMove = undefined;
    if (this.hitTest(_root.dropTarget_mc)) {
        this._x = _root.dropTarget_mc._x+(_root.dropTarget_mc._width/2)-(this._width/2);
        this._y = _root.dropTarget_mc._y+(_root.dropTarget_mc._height/2)-(this._height/2);
        this.gotoAndStop(2);
    } else {
        this.gotoAndStop(1);
    }
};
```

A couple of things are now going to happen when the user releases the mouse. First there is a command to stop dragging. The user has released the mouse, so there will be no more dragging action. The next line releases the updateAfterEvent function that's attached to the mouse move; this is done by setting **this.onMouseMove** equal to null or undefined.

But we want to know where the dragged Object was when it was released, that is to say, where it was dropped. Did it drop within the gray rectangle, the area defined by the hot spot? Or did it drop on a different place on the screen?

The If/Else Statement

The next lines of code set up an if/else statement that will ask the program to check if Hit Test has detected a collision. Specifically, this line of direction means: "Look at me (**this**) and look at my Hit Test method; tell me if it returns the value that indicates that I have overlapped or intersected with the other Movie Clip on the Stage called dropTarget_mc."

Notice we now have open brackets and closed brackets, with an open bracket at the end. Should if equal true, the actions specified within the first set of brackets will be executed. Should if equal false, the program moves on to else portion of the statement and executes an entirely different set of actions as specified within the second pair of brackets.

The logic and the syntax are pretty simple so far. But in this tutorial, you are going to add a bit more user interactivity so that several things happen to reward the user for a successful action.

We want to tell the user, "Yes, you've dropped the Object into the target area successfully." The code between the brackets will cause the Object—our drag_mc Movie Clip—to snap smartly to the exact center of the dropTarget_mc Movie Clip, once the user lets go of the mouse.

The Center Snap

To find the center of dropTarget_mc, we need to indicate the value for the center of the target area. Rather than hard-code those numbers, we'll describe them with generic code.

Let's take a closer look at these two lines:

```
this._x = _root.dropTarget_mc._x+(_root.dropTarget_mc._width/2)-(this._width/2);
this._y = _root.dropTarget_mc._y+(_root.dropTarget_mc._height/2)-(this._height/2);
```

To move the drag_mc Movie Clip (now represented by the generic name **this**) to the exact center of the target area, we first need to find the center points of both its named target area (dropTarget_mc) and that of the moving Object (**this**). Because the program knows how to locate only the coordinates for the top left corner of any Object, we need to ask the program to make some calculations for us.

These directions say, "Move the x position of **this** to a new location." Next, the directions tell the program how to find that location: "Go to the Stage, tell me where the Movie Clip dropTarget_mc is on the x axis and where it is on the y axis. Once you know this, help me find its center." The program finds the center by measuring how wide it is (_width) and dividing that width by 2, and by measuring how high it is (_height) and dividing its height by 2.

We're also asking the program to subtract from these numbers the width and height of drag_mc. This width and height also must be divided by 2 to find the center. In the online tutorial, the Object is 100×100, for example, so dividing by 2 would find the correct center point of 50 and 50.

All these two lines do are find the center points of both Objects, and then match these center points. Because this code is dynamic, it doesn't matter where the target is, and it doesn't matter how big the target is. It doesn't even matter how big the moving Object is. *With these calculations, the code can find the center points of any two Objects and line them up.*

While the code for the calculation looks a bit long, this is very simple, and it adds a bit of sophistication to the drag-and-drop movement. Now the minute the user drops the Object on the target, it will quickly calculate both center points, and snap the Object quickly to the center of the target.

The next line

```
this.gotoAndStop(2);
```

affects the color change described earlier. Now, the little gray box will not only snap to the center of the bigger box, it will also turn a lighter shade of gray. It's another useful visual reinforcement, to let the user know the action has successfully taken place.

The last lines of code define what will happen if an intersection has not taken place, in other words, if the user dropped the Object someplace that does not overlap or intersect with the target hot spot. And what if the user just drags it all around the screen and never bothers to drop it on the target and then release it?

That's when the else plan kicks in. And that's when Hit Test proves its worth.

In this example, if Hit Test detects no overlaps or intersections of the two Movie Clips, nothing much will happen. The else option defaults back to Frame 1, and the box remains its original shade of medium gray. But Hit Test remains at the ready. The minute the Object is dropped onto the target, it will change color and snap to the target coordinates. And as quickly as the user drags it out of the target area and releases, it will jump back and play Frame 1 and turn the gray box darker again.

Setting Multiple Target Areas

In this exercise, an else/if argument does not exist, but that doesn't mean you couldn't add other options. For example, what if you had four targeted drop areas, four different hot spots on the screen?

Setting up collision detection for multiple targets is very simple. The first part of the code stays the same: We ask Hit Test, "Well, did the user drop it?"

The next lines define the options: "If the Object was dropped into a value equal to hot spot A, do this; if it was dropped into hot spot B, do this; if dropped into hot spot C, do this; if it hits hot spot D, do this." And then simply add the else direction: "If it didn't drop on any of the hot spots, *do this*."

The coding sequence for four target areas would look something like this:

```
on (release){
        stopDrag();
    if () {
    } else if (){
    } else if (){
    } else if (){
    } else {
        this.gotoAndStop(1);
    }
}
```

Have fun with this—be imaginative and try different actions/reactions between the brackets of each alternative.

Chapter 10 - Swapping Depths: Z-Sorting

So far in our explorations, we've been working with the x axis and y axis, which are the two-dimensional parameters of Flash screen space. In three-dimensional art programs, there is a third axis: the z axis. Flash is only two-dimensional, but in some cases we can play with images to make them appear to have variable depth in a three-dimensional way. The method that works the best uses a function called *swapDepths*, a capability introduced in Flash 5.

I call this process Z-Sorting, because it is a way to assemble and shuffle visual images so they appear to be stacking positions within a shallow z axis. You can look at the floating menus we built at Kioken for the *Barneys.com* home page to see how this technique can be used to present a lot of information in a way that doesn't clutter up screen real estate.

Barneys.com.

Building the Menu Cards

In this tutorial you will create four rectangular menus. As a user rolls a mouse over the hot spot created for each menu, the menu selected will jump to the forefront of the screen.

1. Begin by creating four rectangles on your screen to represent the menus. In the online tutorial I've made the basic menu card 164×98. To make your own, all you have to do is create one Movie Clip and name it "01 - menu."

2. Duplicate this clip four times on your Stage and give each copy a different instance name, as follows:

   menu_1_mc
   menu_2_mc
   menu_3_mc
   menu_4_mc

3. To allow the user to select and activate each menu individually, you will need to create a hot spot on each of the four menu cards. Create a small, horizontal vector that will cover the top of each menu card—a little sliver or bar. In the web site's version of this tutorial, you'll see that my bar on each menu has the dimensions 160×14. It really is just a sliver, like a header bar.

4. To make the header bar operational, turn that sliver of a vector into a Movie Clip and name it "02 - menuHeader." Give it an instance name of "menuHeader_mc."

Note: If you want to add a shadow, just to give your menus some three-dimensional heft, create a shadow graphic and put it into a third layer now.

Programming the Menu Swaps

Because Z-Sorting counts increments of depth, you need a variable that sets up a base or starting point for counting. We need to define what the "top" will be.

5. On the root Timeline, create a new layer and call it "actions." Now write this code:

```
fscommand ("fullscreen", "false");
fscommand ("allowscale", "false");
stop();

// set a variable to start initial depth
topDepth = 1;
```

This sets up a variable on the stage and makes the variable equal to 1.

To activate the bars, and swap and shuffle the menus around, there will be three actions to execute—after we've hidden the hand cursor icon again. So let's write a little code for the main menu Movie Clip.

6. Go into the Movie Clip 01 – menu. Create a new layer in this Move Clip's own Timeline and call that layer "actions." Write the following code to handle the onPress response:

```
// don't use the hand icon
menuHeader_mc.useHandCursor = false;

// handle onPress event
menuHeader_mc.onPress = function() {
    this._parent.swapDepths(_root.topDepth);
    ++_root.topDepth;
    this._parent.startDrag(false, 26, 25, 549, 172);
    this._parent.onMouseMove = function() {
        updateAfterEvent();
    };
};
```

These lines give the directions to start swapping depths. When the user presses the mouse over the hot spot on any menu's header bar (in effect pressing on the Movie Clip headerBar_mc), this.swapdepths will be equal to the variable of _root.topDepth. When the user presses any header bar for the first time, this.swapdepths is going to equal 1.

This is the starting point. The next line is where we start counting. The plus signs basically mean "add 1." Our topDepth will no longer equal 1, it will equal 2.

From then on, it's a matter of stacking and counting. If the mouse is pressed again, it's going to swap the depth to 2, and topDepth will be equal to 3. Press again, and topDepth will be equal to 4.

These directions also allow the user to drag the menu cards around the screen when pressing down on the mouse; the dragging stops when mouse pressure is released.

7. Now, add the code to handle the onRelease actions:

```
// handle onRelease event
menuHeader_mc.onRelease = menuHeader_mc.onReleaseOutside = function() {
    this._parent.stopDrag();
    this._parent.onMouseMove = undefined;
};
```

Test your movie and see if it works. Whenever a cursor presses upon the hot spot on the header of a menu, that menu should come to the foreground. You should also be able to drag and push the menus around the screen. You can rearrange them at will, and the one that is selected at any given time will present itself to the front.

Implications and Applications

Swapping depths has real value when you need a lot of information on the screen at one time but don't want a lot of clutter. Using it for working assets, such as menus, builds a lot of user-friendliness into a web page, because it lets the user concentrate on a specific element he or she is most interested in, while the rest recede to the background.

And remember, the images that you swap don't have to be menus or anything boring or functional like that. You might create four different animations and have each of them running at the same time. When the user clicks on each in turn, they can be sampled as they are selected; they continue to run even as they are being swapped.

Chapter 11 - Tracking and Custom Cursors: X-Mouse, Y-Mouse

If you visit the web site for *Barneys.com*, you'll notice that the drop-down navigation menus created for the various fashion sections can be separated out, but they will jump back to move with their respective sections if the user shuttles through this squat but wide home page. A little bit of code for the menus lets the menus ask themselves, "Where am I?" And then they look around and say, "I'm totally not in my right place," and a command will be executed to send that menu back to its logically correct place on the screen.

This action is called *tracking*. While the *Barneys.com* site uses a programmatic movement for tracking (see Chapter 17, "Programmatic Movement"), this tutorial will give you a very basic method to track any object on your screen, even as the user moves that object around with the mouse.

The simplest kind of tracking is creating events that respond to the movements of the user's mouse. The _xmouse, _ymouse tracker is actually built into Flash. It is a Property that can at any time evaluate where the current mouse position is.

Using Dynamic Text

Flash has some very cool text capabilities. If you select the Text tool, the Property Inspector will invite you to choose Static, Dynamic, or Input text.

Static text is just that: What you write in Static text is pretty much what you'll always see on the screen. It can't be manipulated any further.

Dynamic text has additional capabilities: It can be assigned a variable name. It provides a field so you can put in the value of a variable, and the text will update in relation to that variable.

With *Input text*, a user can type his name into an input text field, setting the value of a variable. This could then be read in the rest of the document in Dynamic text fields. For example, tailored to that person, "Hi (insert name)!" In this respect, Input text is a little bit like a form field, and it is best used when passing values to the back end.

As soon as you select Dynamic text from the Property Inspector, you'll notice that your text block sprouts a little square handle at the bottom. That's to let you know that you are working in Dynamic text.

If you choose Static text, the handle will appear on top, in the shape of a small circle. That's to remind you that you are working in Static text.

Creating Text Blocks

We're going to create a few text blocks and use them to help track the mouse.

1. Select Dynamic text and use the Type tool to create a text box on your Stage. For the purposes of this tutorial, click the Show Border Around Text Button in the Properties panel so you can see the parameters of your box. If you don't select this, your working area of the text box will be invisible.

2. At the bottom of the Properties panel, you will see an input text field for the name of the variable associated with the text field. Type in **xPos** (shorthand for the x position), which is the name of the first variable. When you have finished, drag that text block to the bottom left of your Stage.

3. It's quicker to create the second text block. Simply highlight the block, press Ctrl+C to copy it, and then press Ctrl+Shift+V, which is the keyboard shortcut for Paste in Place. The Paste in Place command retains the x and y coordinates and places the new text block on top of the first. Hold down the Shift key and use the arrow keys on your keyboard to move the new block below the original one on the Stage.

4. This text box is an exact copy of the previous text box, except one thing has to be changed. In the Properties panels, change xPos to yPos, which stands for y position.

5. Finally, select these two blocks together and press F8 to turn them into a Movie Clip. Name this Movie Clip "01 – inputs." Give it an instance name of "inputs_mc."

Writing the Code

The Event Method we use here is mouseMove, which will execute a function whenever the user moves the mouse.

6. Add a new layer to the root Timeline, name this layer "actions," and write these lines of code:

```
fscommand ("fullscreen", "false");
fscommand ("allowscale", "false");
stop();

// handle "stage" mouseMove event
this.onMouseMove = function() {
    inputs_mc.xPos = Math.floor(_xmouse);
    inputs_mc.yPos = Math.floor(_ymouse);
    updateAfterEvent();
};
```

These are the actions that will be executed each time the user moves the mouse. The code sets the value of the variable xPos to be equal to the current position of the user's mouse on the x axis. The value of the variable yPos will be equal to the current position of the mouse on the y axis. You can use these variables throughout the rest of your content creation.

To test this, go ahead and run the movie. When you move the mouse, the numbers will change in the x and y boxes in the dynamic text fields. This shows you how the program tracks where the mouse is on the Stage, and it automatically shows the mouse position numerically on both the x axis and the y axis.

This example tracks the cursor—the visible point that indicates where the mouse has moved to on the screen. But you can use this technique to track any Object. The only change to the code would be something like this:

```
_root.xPos = Math.floor(_root.myMovieClip_mc._x);
_root.yPos = Math.floor(_root.myMovieClip_mc._y);
```

In both examples, **Math.floor** indicates that the value returned will be rounded to a whole number, instead of a fraction.

Custom Cursors

In this example, we are going to alter the visual image of the cursor as it is moving. It is another way to track the movement of a screen object. The new cursor image will be a set of crosshairs.

1. To start, create a new Movie Clip using a simple piece of vector art—a set of crosshairs. Name the clip "01 - crosshairs."

2. Put a Stop command in the first frame of the Movie Clip's Timeline. While you are in the first frame, change the color of the crosshairs. (I chose white for the online version of this tutorial.)

3. In the second frame, change the color of the crosshairs. (I picked red.)

4. Next, drag your Movie Clip 01 - crosshairs to the Stage and move it offstage, out of the viewable Stage area. Give it an instance name of "crosshairs_mc."

5. Create a new layer on the root Timeline and name the layer "actions." Write these lines of code in the actions layer:

```
fscommand ("fullscreen", "false");
fscommand ("allowscale", "false");
stop();

// hide system mouse pointer
Mouse.hide();
```

This hides the system mouse when the Movie Clip first runs.

6. Now, let's add some more code to be executed whenever the user moves the mouse. Type in:

```
// handle "stage" mouseMove event
this.onMouseMove = function() {
    crosshair_mc._x = _xmouse;
    crosshair_mc._y = _ymouse;
    updateAfterEvent();
};
```

Notice you are no longer targeting a variable; you are targeting where the Movie Clip crosshairs_mc is. Your artwork has replaced the system cursor and will now behave as if it were the system cursor.

Unlike in the earlier tracking tutorial, however, this time there is going to be a bit of a lag between the tracking. If you don't correct it, the tracking will run at the speed of the Movie's specified frames per second rate. In other words, if your movie is running at 12fps, the tracking will also be 12fps. This will manifest itself as a hesitation, or time lag, between the user's mouse movement and what happens on screen.

Adding **updateAfterEvent()** corrects the problem, allowing the tracking function to be performed immediately and independently of the frame rate. This creates a smoother action, and the custom cursor will seem to more or less glide across the screen in response to the user's mouse movements.

The Final Touch

The last element you need to add is a transparent Button.

7. Go on and create a transparent Button (see Chapter 7, "Movie Clips as Buttons and the One Button Trick.")

8. In the Object Actions window for the Button, write this little bit of code:

```
on (rollOver) {
    _root.crosshair_mc.gotoAndStop(2);
}

on (rollOut, dragOut) {
    _root.crosshair_mc.gotoAndStop(1);
}
```

This will allow you to jump frames within that custom cursor Movie Clip. It will let the user know that the cursor is operating, because it is turning from white to red. Run the movie and play with the cursor to see if you've got it right. As soon as you mouse over the hit area of the transparent Button, it should jump from its Frame 1 to Frame 2 and turn from white to red.

Even though the cursor familiar to the system mouse is hidden, users soon adapt to the custom cursor once they discover that manipulating their mouse in a certain way triggers an action on the screen. Changing the crosshairs from white to red informs them that they've hit a hot spot on screen; the natural inclination to continue the interaction (by clicking or dragging the mouse) pulls them further into the adventure you have created.

Chapter 12 - Who Am I? Writing Generic Code

In the earlier chapters of this book, I encouraged you to think of your elements in Flash as Objects, rather than as Symbols or instances. That concept becomes even more important as we move into more complicated work with ActionScript.

ActionScript creates an Object-Oriented Programming (OOP) environment. In terms of Flash, this means we build individual Objects in our projects, and those Objects can act independently of other Objects that will be created later.

As we've learned, we can *talk to* Objects like Movie Clips or Buttons and give them directions about how they will perform on the Stage. But the Objects we target don't have to be static elements. They can be *variables*. Using variables allows us to program Stage actions in ways that will have repercussions far beyond the project we may be doing on any given day.

Variables allow us the advantage of writing generic code. Why write generic code? Because many times you will find yourself writing code that is going to be reused or mutated during the course of a single project or in future projects. Let's say I open up Flash and create a new Movie. I create a new Movie Clip named 01 - blueBox, and I write some code on my root Timeline for this Movie Clip so it will perform a series of actions.

If I didn't think I'd be ever using the blue box code again, I might give it instructions the most direct way possible:

```
_root.blueBox_mc._alpha = 10;
```

This example directs the level of transparency for a blue box Object, in this case with an alpha level of 10 on a scale of 0 to 100.

I finish and move on with my life. Sometime later, I'm building another project for another client and the client says, "Wow, I really liked what you did with that Movie Clip of the blue box. Can you do the same thing for me, only make it a green box and apply it to my green box project?"

Now, one way I could do this is to open the old project, take all the code that I'd written for the blue box and port it to the new green box project. To manage this, I'd have to go through *all* the code, checking for all the times my directions had addressed the blue box and changing them to address the new Object. In other words, I would need to find and change every single **_root.blueBox_mc** to **_root.greenBox_mc**.

Now this really isn't efficient.

I'll have to do the same thing all over again if some other client wants to see the code applied to another Movie Clip within a project about a red box.

The better solution is to create smarter code. Literally. What you want to do is write code that is *self-aware*.

The first step to writing smarter and more generic code is to isolate your directions—your code—away from the other elements in your movie, so that it can be easily plucked out and used again elsewhere. So, don't put your Object-specific code on the root Timeline. Put your code for actions within the Movie Clip instead.

Writing generic code is one of the best methods we can use to switch the "driver" from one "car" to another. With our mind's eye on future projects, we're going to consider the car to be something that will be variable. And we are going to give the driver some smart code so he can drive any sort of variable—for example, any sort of car.

I suggest that you make all of your code generic and, hence, reusable. Earlier in this book we talked about building foundations for your work with Flash. Writing generic code means you never have to reinvent the wheel or continue to do the drudge work of writing the same old code you wrote six months ago.

This allows you to build a library of modules within your foundation that you can reuse quickly when appropriate to save time, and it frees you to create new and more challenging experiences.

Part II - Projects: Intermediate and Advanced Projects

Chapter 13 - Friction

This intermediate-level project, split over two chapters, applies the principle of friction to a moving Object in four ways, all based on the same fundamental code.

The tutorial on the book's web site shows all four variations, which illustrate how the speed and motion of an Object (such as a simple scrollbar) can be affected by programmed calculations that will speed up or slow down the movement. My inspiration for the project was the Shockwave user interface on **www.frogdesign.com**. For their web site, frog design created a huge piece of art that users can shuttle back and forth to display several elements. The effect is very cool because the movements mimic normal physics. The shuttle speeds up at first and then slows down. And when the art smacks up against one end of the display, it bounces back from the impact.

I like this concept: You can assign a program to grab something, and mathematically control how you throw it and what the speed of the Object will be. Just as in the real world, an Object might initially accelerate from the thrust of your throw, but then its speed would start to decrease because of friction. If it hit a barrier, it would bounce back.

So in this project, we will mathematically assign how a user can "grab and throw" an Object on the screen, and write a program that not only controls the speed of the throw, but also the amount of friction we can apply to the Object's speed. This in turn dictates how far and how fast the Object will travel.

We need only two Objects. The first Object will be a Movie Clip that contains the art that will be thrown by the user. In this tutorial, the Object to be thrown will be a scrollbar. The second Object, which I consider to be a valuable element on its own, is what I call a *bounding box*. It is a Movie Clip that will constrain the movements of the thrown Object to the limits of a bounding box. In this tutorial, the bounding box for the scrollbar will be a narrow and gutter-like strip across the screen.

The Bounding Box Concept

In my living room I have a wooden table that has a raised edge along the top four sides. The edge acts like a sort of boundary for the surface of the table. If I were to roll an orange around on the table, it wouldn't fall onto the floor because the raised edge would act as a barrier and keep it within bounds.

The relationship between the orange and the table is interesting because the table can affect the movements of the orange, but both objects are completely independent. The orange is not a part of or within the table; it is merely on the surface of the table. Yet, its movements can be constrained by the table's four raised sides.

The orange says, "Oh, what's beneath me? Okay, a table with four raised sides, so I can never go off the surface of the table."

When I create a bounding box for a moving Object in Flash, I use the same concept: The moving Object (like the orange) contains all the code and is completely independent. But when it is placed "on top of" another Object (like the table) that will act as a bounding box, it can ask, like the orange, "What's beneath me?" Its code will evaluate the dimensions of the boundaries it discovers, and then execute a movement within those screen coordinates.

Building a Bounding Box for a Scrollbar

The first step is to construct a bounding box and give it some coordinates.

1. Take the Rectangle tool, turn Line Art off, and draw a rectangle. While this code is generic and a bounding box may be any size, if you want to follow the web site's online tutorial, make the width 673 and the height 17.

2. Press F8, and turn the rectangle into a Movie Clip. In your Library, name it "02 - scrollbarGutter." Give it an instance name of "scrollbarGutter_mc."

One Object down, one to go.

Creating the Scrollbar

Now that we've created the boundaries that will define the movement of the scrollbar, we can build the scrollbar itself.

3. Again, using the Rectangle tool with Line Art off, draw a rectangle. In the online tutorial, I created a vector with a width of 100 and a height of 15, and I colored it light gray.

4. Press F8, and turn this into a Movie Clip. In your Library, name it "01 - scrollbar." Give it an instance name of "scrollbar_mc."

5. Double-click the 01 - scrollbar Movie Clip to open up its independent Timeline. Name the bottom layer "scrollbar_mc." Create a second layer above this, and name the new layer "actions."

Now we will write the code that sets up commands for what will happen when the user does a press-and-release of his mouse on the gray rectangle of the scrollbar. In sequence, this code will

- Evaluate and return the coordinates of the narrow gutter that will serve as the bounding box

- Monitor the dragging action of the user's mouse as it is being pressed

- Establish the friction and the speed of the throw that occurs after the scrollbar has been pressed and then released

Start by writing the code to evaluate the bounding box.

6. Write the following lines code in the actions layer of the Timeline for the 01 - scrollbar Movie Clip:

```
// set up gutter info
gutterLeft = _root.scrollbarGutter_mc._x+1;
gutterRight = _root.scrollbarGutter_mc._x+_root.scrollbarGutter_mc._width-this._width-1;
```

The first two lines of code set the parameters of the bounding box: how far it can travel left and right within its gutter. We don't need to set a top or bottom parameter, because the scrollbar is only going to be able to move left or right. It won't be going up or down. Top and bottom are the same coordinates in this example. We tell this Movie Clip, "Go to the Stage, find the Movie Clip called scrollbarGutter_mc, and evaluate its coordinates on the x axis." The statement

```
gutterLeft = _root.scrollbarGutter_mc._x+1;
```

sets a variable that will be equal to the position of the Movie Clip scrollbarGutter_mc on the x axis, but plus one.

Why plus one? Because we don't want the scrollbar to reach the exact left edge of its gutter. We want it to be just one increment off. If it were flush, you would not be able to see the boundary. Giving the moving Object that little bit of air space is a design decision that simply makes the boundary clearer for the user to see.

Setting the variable for the right edge of the bounding box is a little bit trickier. The statement

```
gutterRight = _root.scrollbarGutter_mc._x+_root.scrollbarGutter_mc._width-this._width-1;
```

not only sets the right side parameter, it must also take into account the width of the scrollbar. To do this, the program needs to know three things:

- Where is the bounding box on the x axis?
- How wide is the bounding box on the x axis?
- How wide is the scrollbar, minus an increment of one?

So this statement takes into account the size, or more specifically the available running space, of the bounding box. The size of the scrollbar also needs to be evaluated, but its specific size doesn't matter. This is generic code, and we want it to work with any size Object and any size bounding box.

Friction and the Throwing Motion

Now that we've established the boundaries for the scrollbar's movements, we can add the code to execute the movement.

7. Add these lines to the actions layer of the Timeline for the 01 - Scrollbar Movie Clip:

```
// set initial variables
FRICTION = .9;
RATIO = .5;
dragging = false;
// handle onEnterFrame event
this.onEnterFrame = function() {
if (!dragging) {
    oldxpos = this._x;
    newxpos = oldxpos+xSpeed;
    xSpeed *= FRICTION;
    if (newxpos>gutterRight || newxpos<gutterLeft) {
        xSpeed *= -FRICTION;
        newxpos = oldxpos;
    }
    this._x = newxpos;
} else {
    oldxpos = newxpos;
    newxpos = this._x;
}
};
```

Here, the variables FRICTION and RATIO are defined. After that, the Event Method enterFrame sets up the rest of the action in a continuous loop.

Let's go through the variables to explain each one. For example, FRICTION is set at .9.

If FRICTION had been set to equal 1, there would be no decay at all. The Object's speed would remain the same, and there would be no realistic throw, release, and slow-down action. If we rolled around that orange on the table, it would never slow down. If we had set FRICTION to 1.1, however, the Object (the orange) would slowly begin to accelerate. If we set FRICTION equal to 2, it would speed up considerably. Setting FRICTION equal to .9 means there will be a gentle slowing down; the movement has a slight decay.

> **Note: You are probably wondering why, all of a sudden in this syntax, FRICTION is written in all capital letters. That is because FRICTION is going to be a variable that will be used globally throughout this entire movie. The variable RATIO will also be global.**

The number assigned for RATIO describes the momentum of the Object, how fast it will move upon release. This is how we bestow qualities of mass and weight to the moving scrollbar. Here, we set RATIO equal to .5—a halving of the speed. As soon as the scrollbar is thrown, it will have but half of its momentum. In other words, if I picked up the orange and threw it 100 miles an hour, the minute it was released from my hand, its speed would decrease to 50 miles per hour.

Like FRICTION, RATIO can be modified to accelerate or decrease the speed of moving Objects. While in this case, we want the scrollbar to slow down, these numbers can be totally played with. A ratio of 2, for example, would set an Object off like a slingshot; on the user's press-and-release, it would spring vigorously into the confines of its bounding box.

The If/Else Statement

Let's get back to the line, **dragging = false**, which helps us set up the if/else statement that further controls the actions of the Scrollbar.

The Event Method is an enterFrame command, so it will continue as a loop. It first asks the question: "Is the user dragging or not dragging?"

Now we've just set up **dragging = false**. The if statement, however, uses the syntax of a bang or exclamation point before the variable name (**!dragging**), which also means "not dragging."

In this if/else statement, if Flash determines the Object is not dragging or, in other words, that dragging equals false, it will move along to its programmed loop.

The set of actions this triggers will first track the movement of the scrollbar. The previous position of the scrollbar is defined as the variable oldxpos, which is set as follows:

```
oldxpos = this._x;
```

To find the new position of the scrollbar on the x axis, we define it as this:

```
newxpos = oldxpos + xSpeed
```

We've already defined oldxpos in the previous line. The next line defines what xSpeed will be. It is this:

```
xSpeed *= FRICTION
```

The value of xSpeed is equal to itself, multiplied by the value of FRICTION.

At this point the movement has started; the orange is rolling around the table. The next lines set up the second if/else statement, which describes what happens when the Object gets to a boundary. Here, we want the scrollbar to bounce off the edge of the bounding box and move backward. It should be a realistic motion, for if the rolling orange hit a railing, it would rebound—just as a billiard ball rebounds from the cushion of a billiard table.

To create this effect, we ask two questions to return information to the if query.

- **Is newxpos greater than gutterRight?** In other words, has the x axis position overshot the right boundary's position?
- **Is newxpos less than gutterLeft?** This looks to see if it has overshot the left boundary.

Our next variable, xSpeed, is now going to be a multiple of negative friction, that is **–FRICTION**. That's how we control the movement of the scrollbar backward.

The next lines reset the positions and update the motion. Remember, the action will be constantly running, because we've used enterFrame, which creates a continuous loop.

The last lines of the code execute the movement. This sets up the _x value as equal to newxpos. At this point, we can close the brackets, because this is end of the if directions.

Now we have our else statement. The if described what happens when the scrollbar is not dragging (the actions in response to **dragging = false**), so else describes what happens when **dragging = true**.

If there is dragging going on, we need to calculate exactly where we are on the x axis, so the minute the user lets go, the program knows where to start executing the code for the movements. The location depends on where the user has already moved the scrollbar and at which point the mouse was let go. The lines

```
oldxpos = newxpos;
newxpos = this._x;
```

track the movement and reset the x axis coordinate. Without this tracking, there would be no logic to the movement of the scrollbar in response to the dragging. Adding this tracking with the else means the scrollbar will always be responsive to the actions of the user.

Code for the Press and Release

With the program set up to respond to mouse movement, we are ready to finish off by completing the user interface—the program's response to the pressing and releasing of the mouse.

8. Write these lines above the code for enterFrame (what you've already written in the Timeline of the Movie Clip 01 - Scrollbar):

```
// don't use the hand icon
this.useHandCursor = false;
// handle press event
this.onPress = function() {
    this.startDrag(false, gutterLeft, this._y, gutterRight, this._y);
    dragging = true;
    this.onMouseMove = function() {
        updateAfterEvent();
    };
};
```

Once again we've turned off the user's hand icon.

Because Flash MX lets us use Movie Clips like Buttons, we can write the code for press and release commands directly onto the Timeline of the scrollbar Movie Clip.

Now, when the user presses down upon the scrollbar Movie Clip, it will be dragged, but only according to the directions contained within the parentheses of this statement. False, as it appears here, means we are not locking the Object to center. The rest handles the Property for "constrain to rectangle." To find these constraints, the program will go to the Stage, find the current values of the variables for gutterleft, this._y, gutterRight, and this._y.

Notice that this._y is used again, to give the value for the bottom constraint. That's because the scrollbar is only going to be able to move either left or right; it will not move up or down.

The other function set for onPress deals with mouse movements:

```
this.onMouseMove = function() {
        updateAfterEvent();
    };
};
```

It is placed before we close the bracket and allows the user to move the scrollbar at a speed that's independent of the frames-per-second rate. Now the scrollbar should move fluidly in response to the mouse.

Let's move on now to create the throwing effect that occurs upon onRelease, for what happens when the user releases pressure on the mouse.

9. Add the code below to what you've already written:

```
// handle release event
this.onRelease = this.onReleaseOutside = function() {
    this.onMouseMove = undefined;
    this.stopDrag();
    dragging = false;
    xSpeed = (newxpos-oldxpos)*RATIO;
};
```

On release, we first disable updateAfterEvent on the mouse move. We do this by making it equal to undefined (or null). Then, we give the command to stopDrag; we obviously want to stop dragging that Movie Clip. We then set up a variable that looks to see if, indeed, the Movie Clip is being dragged or not. This is taken care of with **dragging = false**, and provides the input that triggers the code we have already written below.

Notice also that here, xSpeed is a variable that is equal to the Object's current x position, minus its old x position, multiplied by RATIO. This gives an indication of how the user is manipulating the mouse: Has the user moved it softly or moved it quickly and erratically?

If you test this movie, you'll see that dragging will constrain the rectangle to the bounding box it is sitting on top of, just like our orange on the table. When the scrollbar's Movie Clip is pressed and released, it will take off and travel on its own through the gutter. Its motion will decay and slow down, and if the scrollbar hits either the left or right edges of the gutter, it will bounce back with a realistic motion.

Chapter 14 - Friction Variations

The three projects in this chapter are useful variations on the friction theme, adding new capabilities to the basic code you learned in Chapter 13, "Friction." In fact, you can copy that file you just finished to make a new file, because we will be using it again. Just use Save As and give the file a new name. A look at the online tutorial for "Friction, Part II" will show you what the three new variations will look like.

Friction, Part II

Scrollbars, of course, aren't any good unless they move content, so this tutorial has a scrollbar that will move a Movie Clip that can contain art or a block of text. The block of text in this variation will be large enough so it can't be seen on the screen in its entirety. The scrollbar will allow the user to shuttle the Movie Clip back and forth so portions of the content may be viewed at a time.

When the file starts, the scrollbar and the copy on screen are both aligned to the left. When the scrollbar is activated and moved to the right, the text block will move in the opposite direction, further off to the left. If the scrollbar continues to be moved to the right, the copy will continue moving left until it enters a "nonviewable" area of the screen.

Working with Copy Blocks and Text

One of the project's first decisions is how to create the text for the Movie Clip. Use Flash's Vector tool, and the program will run excruciatingly slow because it must move each vector point for each character. For example, even in a short word such as "the," there are a lot of vectors and points that make up the shapes of the individual letters. So any movement will be choppy: The program must chug along as it attempts to render every single letter of every single word.

Of course, the file size might only be 4K. But what you gain in simplicity, you lose in performance when you rely on vectors for text.

So, what's the fix? My fix is to do all my text in Photoshop, then export it as a GIF, which will keep the type crisp. Next, I import that GIF into Flash and turn it into a Movie Clip. If you don't have Photoshop, you can use any of the numerous photo-manipulative programs available that do the same thing.

Of course, if your text is an imported graphic, your file size will no longer be a compact 4KB. It might be as big as 30KB, because it's an image created with pixel art. In this case, I'm willing to live with a bigger file size because it makes life easier for the scrollbar. All the scrollbar has to do is move a Movie Clip back and forth.

One tip: When I export text as a GIF, I use a transparent background, so only the typeface appears. Knocking out the background of the text makes it possible to add other images behind the text, to create an independent background that can provide a sense of layering or depth. We'll try this later in the "Friction, Part III" section.

Building the Scrollable Copy Block

Once you've copied the scrollbar Movie Clip on your Stage, you can add the second element, which will be your own copy block.

1. Create some text in a pixel-based program (Photoshop, for example) and export it as a GIF. Import the GIF into Flash and turn it into a Movie Clip. Name it "03 - content."

2. Put this Movie Clip on the Stage and give it an instance name of "content_mc."

Now we'll add two short lines of code to the Movie Clip 01 - Scrollbar. We've already got it looking outside of itself to find the parameters of its gutter, or bounding box. Now it will look to find and control the block of copy as well.

3. Open up 01 - scrollbar and add the highlighted lines of code on the Movie Clip's actions layer, above the original gutter information:

```
// set up content_mc info
contentRight = _root.content_mc._x;
contentLeft = 715-_root.content_mc._width;
// set up gutter info
gutterLeft = _root.scrollbarGutter_mc._x+1;
gutterRight = _root.scrollbarGutter_mc._x+_root.scrollbarGutter_mc._width-this._width-1;
```

These lines look at contentRight and contentLeft, which are the parameters of how far the copy block can move right and left, respectively. Here, contentRight describes the copy block's starting location. The contentLeft variable will be equal to our viewable screen, minus the width of the content Movie Clip.

The press-and-release instructions are the same as in Chapter 13's friction project:

```
// don't use the hand icon
this.useHandCursor = false;
// handle press event
this.onPress = function() {
    this.startDrag(false, gutterLeft, this._y, gutterRight, this._y);
    dragging = true;
    this.onMouseMove = function() {
        updateAfterEvent();
    };
};
// handle release event
this.onRelease = this.onReleaseOutside = function() {
    this.onMouseMove = undefined;
    this.stopDrag();
    dragging = false;
    xSpeed = (newxpos-oldxpos)*RATIO;
};
```

4. Our only other amendment is to the event Method enterFrame. In this case we add two lines of code in two places. Add the highlighted code to the if statement and also to the else statement, as indicated:

```
// set initial variables
FRICTION = .9;
RATIO = .5;
dragging = false;

// handle onEnterFrame event
this.onEnterFrame = function() {
    if (!dragging) {
        oldxpos = this._x;
        newxpos = oldxpos+xSpeed;
        xSpeed *= FRICTION;
        if (newxpos>gutterRight || newxpos<gutterLeft) {
            xSpeed *= -FRICTION;
            newxpos = oldxpos;
        }
        this._x = newxpos;
        // always move content_mc whether dragging or not
        var percent = (this._x-gutterLeft)/(gutterRight-gutterLeft);
        this._parent.content_mc._x = percent*(contentLeft-contentRight)+contentRight;
    } else {
        oldxpos = newxpos;
        newxpos = this._x;
        // always move content_mc whether dragging or not
        var percent = (this._x-gutterLeft)/(gutterRight-gutterLeft);
        this._parent.content_mc._x = percent*(contentLeft-contentRight)+contentRight;
    }
}
```

These new lines of code tell the Movie Clip content_mc to move in the opposite direction that the Movie Clip scrollbar_mc is moving. In other words, when the user moves the scrollbar to the right, the text block will move to the left.

What we've done is introduce a local variable using the syntax **var percent**. This variable maps the movement as an inverse percentage, proportionate to the width of both Movie Clips. The movement of the content will be executed as a percentage of its width to the scrollbar's width, compared to the available room it has to move in.

> **Note: There are two different types of variables: global variables and local variables.** A *global variable* can be called from anywhere within the entire movie. Its value remains constant, and it never expires. For example:
>
> ```
> _root.Joshua = 1;
> ```
>
> means that Joshua will always be equal to 1 and can always be called.
>
> *Local variables* are declared using the Flash keyword var, as in
>
> ```
> var Joshua = x –y;
> ```
>
> and only come into existence when a certain direction is executed. When the executed program is finished, the variables— and the values they had—just expire.

Here, we specify **var percent** to make the variable named percent equal to where the Scrollbar Movie Clip is on the x axis minus gutterLeft, then divided by gutterRight minus gutterLeft. We're making this a local variable, rather than a hard number, and including in this calculation the size of the content. This makes the code entirely dynamic, because the scrollbar or the content may not always start at 0. (In the online tutorial, for example, I've used a small offset.)

For example, if the width of the content were 200 and the width of the scrollbar were 100, every time the scrollbar moved 10 pixels in one direction, the content would move 20 pixels in the opposite direction. In fact, it doesn't matter how wide your content is. It could be a mile wide and the code would still work, because the movement will be proportional with this very simple equation.

The subsequent line moves the x axis position of the content_mc Movie Clip in reverse proportion to the x axis position of the moving scrollbar_mc Movie Clip.

We add these lines to the else statement as well as to the if statement, because we want the reverse action to occur not only as a rapid shuttle on a press, but as a slow, frictioned glide in both directions when the scrollbar is pressed and then released.

Friction, Part III

This variation introduces a background for the text created in the last project. This background is created as a separate Movie Clip, so it can be programmed to move in relationship to the scrollbar, but may move independently of it.

If you try the online tutorial for this project, you'll notice that the background moves at a slower rate than the copy block. Two different Movie Clips, each linked to scrollbar activities but moving at different speeds, create an interesting, almost three-dimensional effect.

Adding Background Art

Once again, you'll be building on what you've already created, so copy the file for "Friction, Part II" and save it as "Friction Part, III." We'll just be adding on to the Movie Clips from the earlier project.

1. Create some pixel-based background art in Photoshop or a similar program. Export it as a GIF, and then import that GIF into Flash and put it into a Movie Clip. Make its width slightly smaller than the text block Movie Clip, but make sure it is the same height.

2. Name this new Movie Clip "04 - contentBG." Give it an instance name of "contentBG_mc."

3. To affect this new background Movie Clip, we only need to a few more lines of new code inside the scrollbar Movie Clip. So, open up the Movie Clip 01 - scrollbar. Open the actions layer in its Timeline, and insert the highlighted lines of code between the setups for the content and the gutter:

```
// set up content_mc info
contentRight = _root.content_mc._x;
contentLeft = 715-_root.content_mc._width;

// set up contentBG_mc info
contentBGRight = _root.contentBG_mc._x;
contentBGLeft = 715-_root.contentBG_mc._width;
// set up gutter info
gutterLeft = _root.scrollbarGutter_mc._x+1;
gutterRight = _root.scrollbarGutter_mc._x+_root.scrollbarGutter_mc._width-this._width-1;
```

Notice this is exactly the same code we used for the moving copy blocks. We're applying the same instructions to the movement of the background.

4. Press-and-release instructions are the same, but now we will add a single new line each to the enterFrame's if and else statements. Again, add the highlighted code:

```
// don't use the hand icon
this.useHandCursor = false;
// handle press event
this.onPress = function() {
    this.startDrag(false, gutterLeft, this._y, gutterRight, this._y);
    dragging = true;
    this.onMouseMove = function() {
        updateAfterEvent();
    };
};
```

```
// handle release event
this.onRelease = this.onReleaseOutside = function() {
    this.onMouseMove = undefined;
    this.stopDrag();
    dragging = false;
    xSpeed = (newxpos-oldxpos)*RATIO;
};
// handle onEnterFrame event
this.onEnterFrame = function() {
    if (!dragging) {
        oldxpos = this._x;
        newxpos = oldxpos+xSpeed;
        xSpeed *= FRICTION;
        if (newxpos>gutterRight || newxpos<gutterLeft) {
            xSpeed *= -FRICTION;
            newxpos = oldxpos;
        }
        this._x = newxpos;
        // always move content_mc whether dragging or not
        var percent = (this._x-gutterLeft)/(gutterRight-gutterLeft);
        this._parent.content_mc._x = percent*(contentLeft-contentRight)+contentRight;
        this._parent.contentBG_mc._x = percent*(contentBGLeft-contentBGRight)+contentBGRight;
    } else {
        oldxpos = newxpos;
        newxpos = this._x;
        // always move content_mc whether dragging or not
        var percent = (this._x-gutterLeft)/(gutterRight-gutterLeft);
        this._parent.content_mc._x = percent*(contentLeft-contentRight)+contentRight;
        this._parent.contentBG_mc._x = percent*(contentBGLeft-contentBGRight)+contentBGRight;
    }
};
```

Adding just four new lines of code allows the scrollbar to control this new element. We don't have to reiterate the local variable we named "percent," because it will apply to the movement of both elements. Yet their movements will look different. The three-dimensional effect occurs simply because the background Movie Clip is a different size than the content Movie Clip. It is smaller, so the percentage values of its movements are proportionately different: It will move slower.

Friction, Part IV

As you can see, the elements you are creating are completely modular. This code can be copied to make many different onscreen Objects move in relation to a user interface. That said, it should be no surprise that our next variation involves building three different rows of content on screen, each one with its own independent scrollbar. If you access the online tutorial for this variation, you'll see what the finished product looks like.

This may look complicated, but it uses the same engine we used for the first friction project in Chapter 13.

Embedding a Scrollbar Within a Copy Block

If you look at the online tutorial for this variation, you'll see that the scrollbar *is* the content. Notice that the gutters have been removed; we will create a different kind of bounding box for the moving elements.

1. Begin by opening the file you created for Chapter 13's friction project. Select just the Movie Clip for the scrollbar, 01 - scrollbar, and copy it for this new project.
2. Copy and paste it three times onto your stage.
3. Give each of the three copies a different instance name:

   scrollbar_1_mc
   scrollbar_2_mc
   scrollbar_3_mc

When we do this, Flash MX thinks we have three different elements, but all we need is just one Movie Clip with its attendant code.

The copies can be placed anywhere on your Stage. In the online tutorial, I placed them in vertical bands. The position of the first copy is x: 26, y: 25. The second is at x: 26, y: 109, and the third is parked at x: 26, y: 193.

4. Create some art or import as a GIF a text block for each of the three copied Movie Clips. In the online tutorial, I used the same text block for all three Movie Clips, but you could certainly create unique content for each of the three. While the text blocks shown in the tutorial have a width of 896, I would suggest you give your content a width of at least 1000 so that you see the resulting movements easily.

Amending the Code in the Scrollbar

Code in the scrollbar_mc Movie Clip will control the movements of all three at the same time. What's different is we no longer need the gutters; the text blocks don't need a visible frame. They are just long images that can be shuttled back and forth, and they serve as their own scrollbars.

5. Here is the new code to write in the actions layer of the Timeline for the 01 - scrollbar_mc Movie Clip:

```
// set up gutter info
gutterRight = this._x;
gutterLeft = 713-this._width;
// don't use the hand icon
this.useHandCursor = false;
// handle press event
this.onPress = function() {
    this.startDrag(false, gutterLeft, this._y, gutterRight, this._y);
    dragging = true;
    this.onMouseMove = function() {
        updateAfterEvent();
    };
};
// handle release event
this.onRelease = this.onReleaseOutside = function() {
    this.onMouseMove = undefined;
    this.stopDrag();
    dragging = false;
    xSpeed = (newxpos-oldxpos)*RATIO;
};
// set initial variables
FRICTION = .9;
RATIO = .5;
```

```
dragging = false;
// handle onEnterFrame event
this.onEnterFrame = function() {
    if (!dragging) {
        oldxpos = this._x;
        newxpos = oldxpos+xSpeed;
        xSpeed *= FRICTION;
        if (newxpos>gutterRight || newxpos<gutterLeft) {
            xSpeed *= -FRICTION;
            newxpos = oldxpos;
        }
        this._x = newxpos;
    } else {
        oldxpos = newxpos;
        newxpos = this._x;
    }
};
```

In our earlier versions, the very first lines of code set up the gutter information. In this variation, we will still set up gutterRight and gutterLeft, but now gutterRight will be equal to this._x, its starting position, and gutterLeft will be equal to the width of the moveable viewable area, minus the Movie Clip's own width. The copy blocks look at their own positions, and we're only constraining their movement to the size of the viewable area.

Even without a visible frame, a bounding box can restrict the movement of an Object, which in this case acts as a self-scrollbar. Pressing and releasing the mouse upon the copy blocks will make them travel to the left or the right, and they'll slow down gracefully to a stop when the mouse is released.

This project is just one way to move large blocks of content on your screen, so experiment with additional variations. For example, in this tutorial I didn't provide visible boundaries simply as a design decision. You could create gutters or boundaries visible to the viewer; use the code for Chapter 13's bounding box, and merely change the numbers for top, right, and left to adjust for the larger area of movement.

⬆UP
LOADING | IN THE PROCESS, OF.

"The Process" 1999 . Moveable timeline.

001	**002**	**003**
October . 08 . 1999	October . 09 . 1999	October . 10 . 1999
Core Members of Uploading meet in New York	New York Uploading WebJam	What has UPLoading become? Where is it headed?
015	**016**	**017**
November . 18 . 1999	November . 19 . 1999	November . 22 . 1999
PrayStation whispers Antiweb CHAOS	The core is rotting	The status of the " Energy and Development " section
021	**022**	**023**

⬇

In the **Process** of **Development**, the **Energy Inspires Information** resulting in **Communication**

Chapter 15 - Collisions

If you worked your way through the friction tutorials, this project should be a breeze. You will use basically the same engine and build on the foundation laid in the previous two chapters.

In the friction projects, however, our scrollbars and text blocks could move from left to right only; their movements were constrained to a narrow, gutter-like space on the screen. This program is a bit closer to our example of the orange on the table, because the moveable Object will be given a broader range of movement on a broader playing field, and it will react differently when it collides with the coordinates of its bounding box.

For this project, we want the object to be able to move up and down the screen, top to bottom, as well as to move side to side. And when it hits the boundary on any of the four sides of the its bounding box, it will bounce off and travel in the opposite direction.

Creating the Bounding Box

Again, we have only two elements: the Object to be moved and a bounding box.

1. Create a good-sized bounding box (see Chapter 13,"Friction"). In the online collisions tutorial, I used a width of 689 and a height of 247, and aligned the box at the coordinates x: 25, y: 24, rather than at the 0 points.

2. Turn this into a Movie Clip and name it "02 - boundaries." Give it an instance name of "boundaries_mc."

3. Now create the Object that will be thrown around. For the online tutorial, I created a 40×40 rectangle and aligned it to the center of the screen. Name your Object "01 - object."

Remember the analogy of cars and drivers from Chapter 12? Here we are not going to put all the code for the Object's movement on the root Timeline, which, to me, would be like putting all the code inside the parking lot. Instead, we're going to put the code within the object_mc Movie Clip, so it can drive itself around.

4. Open the Timeline of object_mc, create a bottom layer called "vectors," and place the art there. Above this, create a new layer called "actions." In this, write the following code to describe how the Object will move around on the Stage:

```
// set up gutter info
boundaryLeft = _root.boundaries_mc._x + 1;
boundaryRight = ((_root.boundaries_mc._x + _root.boundaries_mc._width) - this._width) - 1;
boundaryTop = _root.boundaries_mc._y + 1;
boundaryBottom = ((_root.boundaries_mc._y + _root.boundaries_mc._height) - this._height) - 1;
```

As in Chapter 13, this code establishes the boundaries for our bounding box. But it's different from the friction code because it sets four variables, not just two. Here we need to set up all four corners, because the moving Object will be able to move up, down, left, and right.

You must take into account not only the x but now the y position of the bounding box. Then you must subtract the Object's width and height, and also add or subtract 1 for the one-pixel buffer on all sides.

This defines the Object's range of movement within your larger bounding box and sets up the press-and-release instructions.

Moving in Four Directions

Because this Object will move up and down as well as left to right, we need take into account these y axis movements when we set up the enterFrame commands. To do this we set a new variable named "ypos," which stands for y position. This, of course, leads us to define oldypos and newypos, as we did with xpos. For every xpos direction, we simply add a ypos direction. And we'll add a new variable called "ySpeed" to address the y axis components needed for FRICTION and RATIO.

5. Add this code for the enterFrame Event Method below what you've already written:

```
// set initial variables
FRICTION = .9;
RATIO = 2;
dragging = false;

// handle onEnterFrame event
this.onEnterFrame = function() {
    if (!dragging) {
        oldxpos = this._x;
        oldypos = this._y;
        newxpos = oldxpos + xSpeed;
        newypos = oldypos + ySpeed;
        xSpeed *= FRICTION;
        ySpeed *= FRICTION;
        if (newxpos>boundaryRight || newxpos<boundaryLeft) {
            xSpeed *= -FRICTION;
            newxpos = oldxpos;
        }
        if (newypos>boundaryBottom || newypos<boundaryTop) {
            ySpeed *= -FRICTION;
            newypos = oldypos;
        }
        this._x = newxpos
        this._y = newypos
    } else {
        oldxpos = newxpos;
        oldypos = newypos;
        newxpos = this._x;
        newypos = this._y;
    }
};
```

This code also makes a few significant changes in how the Object will react when it hits a boundary edge. For one thing, RATIO has increased: It's now equal to 2. This means that when the user propels the Object, the minute the user releases the mouse it is not going to slow down, it is going to accelerate. Initially, it will go at twice the speed it was "thrown," but then this speed will decay as friction is applied.

Adjusting the Press and Release

The last task is to make a slight modification to the user's press-and-release user interface. We want the user to be able to throw or fling the box around, within the confines of the bounding box. If the user presses the Object, the throwing motion will occur on a mouse release, or on releaseOutside.

6. To accomplish this, write the following code in the actions layer of the Timeline for the Movie Clip object_mc. Add the code above the enterFrame directions written earlier:

```
// don't use the hand icon
this.useHandCursor = false;

// handle press event
this.onPress = function() {
    this.startDrag(false, boundaryLeft, boundaryTop, boundaryRight, boundaryBottom);
    dragging = true;
    this.onMouseMove = function() {
        updateAfterEvent();
    };
};

// handle release event
this.onRelease = this.onReleaseOutside = function() {
    this.onMouseMove = undefined;
    this.stopDrag();
    dragging = false;
    xSpeed = (newxpos-oldxpos) * RATIO;
    ySpeed = (newypos-oldypos) * RATIO;
};
```

Just like the orange on the table, the Object can be thrown to roll around, but it will move only within the confines of the bounding box—our table railings. This file is not only completely generic, it is totally dynamic. The moving Object is sitting on top of another Object, and it will always stay within the confines of what it is sitting on. To change the size of the playing area, all you have to do is resize the bounding box.

Chapter 16 - Wrapping Space

Remember Asteroids, that video game sensation from 1979? In this game from Atari, moving objects could navigate only within the viewable screen space. The game compensated, however, to keep them in play a bit longer. When an asteroid or projectile reached the edge of the screen, it would next appear again by entering on the opposite side, as if it had somehow wrapped or traveled around in a circle offscreen.

This project, another variation of the bounding box, was inspired by Asteroids. In this chapter, we are going to set up directions for what will happen if the Object moves *over* the edge of its bounding box.

This requires setting up four variables that describe what happens if the user wants to drag the Object around on screen: The user will be allowed to drag the Object only within the confines of the bounding box.

The second set of instructions respond to the press and release of the user's mouse—flinging or throwing the Object. When this happens, it will be just like tossing or throwing that orange over the table: The orange might sail over the railing and go over the boundary edge. But, just like in Asteroids, the orange (or the Object) is going to reappear again on the opposite side of the viewable area, as if it had circumnavigated the table in a wrapping motion and popped back up on the other side. Friction techniques will be used to accelerate and then retard the speed of the moving Object.

Return of the Bounding Box

We'll begin by building the bounding box. At this point, you might want to view the web site's online tutorial for this project to see how the completed project looks.

1. Start by copying the whole file you created in Chapter 15, "Collisions," and save it as a new file. All we're really going to do is delete some instructions, and add a few more lines.

2. Open the actions layer of the Timeline for the Movie Clip object_mc, and amend the code by adding some new code prior to the onEnterFrame directions and a final line within the onEnterFrame function. The lines to add are highlighted below:

```
// set up gutter info
boundaryLeft = _root.boundaries_mc._x + 1;
boundaryRight = ((_root.boundaries_mc._x + _root.boundaries_mc._width) - this._width) - 1;
boundaryTop = _root.boundaries_mc._y + 1;
boundaryBottom = ((_root.boundaries_mc._y + _root.boundaries_mc._height) - this._height) - 1;
// don't use the hand icon
this.useHandCursor = false;
// handle press event
this.onPress = function() {
    this.startDrag(false, boundaryLeft, boundaryTop, boundaryRight, boundaryBottom);
    dragging = true;
    this.onMouseMove = function() {
        updateAfterEvent();
    };
};

// handle release event
this.onRelease = this.onReleaseOutside = function() {
    this.onMouseMove = undefined;
    this.stopDrag();
    dragging = false;
    xSpeed = (newxpos-oldxpos) * RATIO;
    ySpeed = (newypos-oldypos) * RATIO;
};

// set initial variables
FRICTION = .9;
RATIO = 2;
dragging = false;
```

```
function wrapSpace() {
    // evaluate the space and adjust object accordingly
    if (this._x<boundaryLeft - this._width) {
        this._x = boundaryRight+(this._width);
    } else {
        if (this._x>boundaryRight + this._width) {
            this._x = boundaryLeft-(this._width);
        }
    }
    if (this._y<boundaryTop - this._height) {
        this._y = boundaryBottom+(this._height);
    } else {
        if (this._y>boundaryBottom + this._height) {
            this._y = boundaryTop-(this._height);
        }
    }
}

// handle onEnterFrame event
this.onEnterFrame = function() {
    if (!dragging) {
        oldxpos = this._x;
        oldypos = this._y;
        newxpos = oldxpos + xSpeed;
        newypos = oldypos + ySpeed;
        xSpeed *= FRICTION;
        ySpeed *= FRICTION;
        this._x = newxpos
        this._y = newypos
        wrapSpace();
    } else {
        oldxpos = newxpos;
        oldypos = newypos;
        newxpos = this._x;
        newypos = this._y;
    }
};
```

There are a lot of similarities to the collisions project here. FRICTION is still equal to .9 and RATIO is still 2, to control speed and momentum. Dragging still equals false.

But the onEnterFrame code is different. And as you've probably noticed, something is missing from our if and else statements. The x and y coordinates for the boundaries have been stripped out. So how will the program determine where the Object is? How does it determine whether the Object has passed a boundary at all? And what does it do if a boundary is passed?

The wrapSpace Function

Our solution is to give the directions to set up and launch a function, just prior to the onEnterFrame directions. The wrapSpace function evaluates the space and adjusts the Object's movement accordingly. Here is the necessary code in detail:

```
function wrapSpace() {

    if (this._x<boundaryLeft - this._width) {
        this._x = boundaryRight+(this._width);
    } else {
        if (this._x>boundaryRight + this._width) {
            this._x = boundaryLeft-(this._width);
        }
    }
    if (this._y<boundaryTop - this._height) {
        this._y = boundaryBottom+(this._height);
    } else {
        if (this._y>boundaryBottom + this._height) {
            this._y = boundaryTop-(this._height);
        }
    }
}
```

The wrapSpace function first checks to see if an Object wants to wrap—in other words, if it has gone past the boundary edge and is ready to come up again on the other side. It checks all four edges, using if/else statements.

Notice the math symbols for less than and greater than have been included in each. Take a closer look at the first if statement to examine the syntax:

```
if (this._x<boundaryLeft - this._width) {
        this._x = boundaryRight+(this._width);
```

This if statement says, "Find out if the x position of the Object is *less than* the x position of the Left boundary, minus the Object's width. Is it still within the left side of the boundary, or has it gone beyond it?"

The code then checks all boundaries with the four if statements. Once it has determined that the Object has moved past at least one boundary edge, the rest of the code executes the wrap. It will now reset the Object's x and y positions and make it appear on the opposite side.

The Object, however, will continue to move at the speed and momentum at which it was originally thrown. Friction still occurs, and the Object slows down consistently. This use of friction gives the indication that this is the same thrown Object whose movement has continued. (We don't need a direction for "negative friction," as in the Collisions project, because the Object does not bounce, it just moves forward when thrown.)

Having defined the function for wrapSpace in these lines, all that's left is to call the function at the end of the onEnterFrame directions. This function will constantly monitor any boundary breach caused by a press-and-release, calculate the logical point of reappearance, and complete the wrap.

Run this movie to see the results. If you drag the box around the play area, it should stay within the confines of the bounding box built for it. If a press-and-release action initiates a throw, the Object should disappear offscreen, and then reappear onscreen from the opposite direction. If thrown to the right, the object should reappear on the left; if thrown to the bottom, it should re-enter from the top. The momentum of the Object should remain the same.

Chapter 17 - Programmatic Movement

In this tutorial, you'll learn one of several methods of using ActionScript to make an Object move in relation to another Object. The first project programs actions in relation to a static Object, or *Marker*; a second variation programs actions in relation to a Marker that may also be moved.

There are only two elements: two Movie Clips. The first Movie Clip contains the Object that will be moving; the second Movie Clip contains the Marker. The code that enables the Object to find the Marker and move toward it is placed on the root Timeline.

Walking in Math Class

I never paid much attention to math in school, but I'm a visual guy and one particular lesson has stuck with me. The teacher proposed an interesting problem:

> "If I were standing at one side of the classroom and another person were standing at the other side of the classroom, and if I could travel half the distance between us in each step, when would I reach the other person? If the distant person were twenty feet away, and I moved ten feet in the first step, five feet in the second step, two-and-a-half feet in the next step, and so on?"

The question, the paradigm, was this: Would the teacher ever really reach and touch the other person? Now in mathematics, the answer is no. The teacher would never reach the other person, even though the last steps would be microscopically small, because math is infinite. Dividing a distance by half is a calculation that goes on infinitely, well beyond the decimal point.

In the case of Flash, however, once you get to a certain place beyond the decimal point the math gives up, so one Object would eventually hit the other Object. But the problem itself inspired this tutorial, where an Object will move programmatically, calculating half the distance as it goes.

Sliding Object and Static Marker

The web site's online tutorial for this project shows how a box-like Object can be moved in relation to a static Object. The static Object serves as its reference point.

1. Draw a 100×100 rectangular vector on the Stage. Select it and press F8 to turn it into a Movie Clip. Name the Movie Clip "01 - sliding Object." Give it an instance name of "slidingObject_mc."

2. Draw a smaller 20×20 rectangular vector on the Stage. If you're following the online tutorial, fill it with a light gray color. Select it and press F8 to turn it into a Movie Clip. Name this Movie Clip "02 - marker." Give it an instance name of "marker_mc."

3. Position both Movie Clips as the starting point for any action. In the online tutorial, I aligned the slidingObject_mc Movie Clip to a position that is 55 on the x axis, and 140 on the y axis. I positioned my marker_mc Movie Clip at 584 on the x axis, and I gave it a y axis position of 54.

I should mention that when I'm working on a finished project, I generally position the marker not on the Stage but in the offstage working area, so it's not visible. All the user sees is the Object moving—little do they know there is a Marker offscreen to control its actions. For the purposes of this tutorial, we put both the moving Object and its Marker on the viewable part of the Stage.

Adding the User Interface

The next phase of the project is to add a Transparent Button for the user interface.

4. Now, create a new layer of the root Timeline. Name this layer, "text." With your Text tool, add the words **Press Me To Slide Object**.

5. Add another layer to the Timeline, and call it "button." Drag out the transparent Button from your Library (the same one we used for the basic tutorials), and place it over the words that you've written. If necessary, resize the Transparent Button to fit the length of the words.

6. The Button will trigger the actions and serve as your user interface. So, highlight the Button, open up the Actions frame, and write the following code:

```
on (press) {
_root.running = true;
}
```

This means that on the pressing action, the program will go to the Stage and set a variable called **running** equal to **true**.

Code for the Programmed Movement

All of the movements in response to the Button press are written in the root Timeline. Like the other elements we've just created, the code is modular and can be used with any variety of moving Objects, Markers, or Buttons for your own projects.

7. Open up the root Timeline, create a new layer, and name it "actions." In this layer, write the code that will perform the movement of the slide:

```
fscommand ("fullscreen", "false");
fscommand ("allowscale", "false");
stop();

// handle onEnterFrame event

_root.slidingObject_mc.onEnterFrame = function() {
    if (_root.running && Math.abs(_root.marker_mc._x-this._x)<1) {
        // set position and hang out
        this._x = _root.marker_mc._x;
        _root.running = false;
    } else if (_root.running) {
        this._x -= (this._x-_root.marker_mc._x)*.5;
    } else {
        // wait for button press
    }
};
```

To execute the movement and reposition our sliding Object, an Event Method, onEnterFrame, runs a function that examines the location of the Object, looks at the location of its Marker, and calculates not only the distance between the two but the speed required as well. This is done as a statement series of an if, an else/if, and an else. In the if statement, Math.abs means the value returned is an absolute number that disregards whether it happens to be a positive or negative number. (In other words, if we're at 0, and take two steps forward, that would be +2. Two steps backward would be –2, but Math.abs would read both merely as 2.)

In this if statement, Math.abs is being used to determine whether the sliding Object is *at least one pixel away* from its Marker. If this is found to be true, the code will "lock" _slidingObject_mc to the same position as marker_mc.

Naturally, when the movie runs for the first time, the if statement is going to fail, because the sliding Object is nowhere near the Marker.

The else/if statement

```
} else if (_root.running) {
```

tells the program what to do if the first if test fails. The else/if kicks in and simply looks to see if running equals true—in other words, whether or not the Button has been pushed.

When this movie runs for the first time, running does not equal true, but a press of the Button sets running to true. Now, the code has a new answer for its if statement. Once it learns that running equals true, it moves the sliding Object toward the Marker.

The movement is calculated and executed in this line:

```
this._x -= (this._x-_root.marker_mc._x)*.5;
```

It is a short, but fairly complex, direction that says, "The Object's x position is equal to itself, minus the difference between the x position of itself and the Movie Clip marker_mc, multiplied by .5." Multiplying by .5 provides the multiple of the speed required for the movement to the new location. Here, the multiple is 50 percent—*half the distance*.

To understand the way we set this speed, think back again to the example of the math class. If I were 100 feet away from the other person, I'd know that half the distance was 50 feet. That would be one step. Half the distance again would be 25 feet, half the distance again 12.5 feet. Now, that's a lot of ground covered in a few short steps. The relative speed is faster at first, but the steps get slower as the distance grows shorter.

Here, the jumps are also half the distance. If the original distance difference on the x axis is 200, the early movement along that axis will be fast, from 200 to 100. From 100 to 50, from 50 to 25, and so on, the speed of the movement slows down as the sliding Object approaches its Marker.

The last section of code looks at what happens when the else/if fails—in other words, if the running variable doesn't equal true. Well, in this case it means that the Button hasn't been pressed, and the program will just hang out and wait until a press occurs.

You can now test your Movie and see how these two Movie Clips evaluate each other. You'll also see where you might want to do some tweaking. For example, in the code you've just written, the variable for speed is the value of distance multiplied by .5. If you run the Movie, this may seem a bit too fast.

So go ahead and change the number. Multiply distance by .2, and you'll get a slower movement, because that's equivalent to only 20%, not half, of the distance, which might provide a more fluid movement. A larger number, such as 1.6, will be so fast that the Object will overshoot the Marker and have to jump backward to get where it's supposed to be. This produces an interesting rubber-band-like movement.

Note also that moving the position of the Marker, of course, changes how and where the sliding Object will move. In your own work, you may find that if a moving Object doesn't move exactly where you want it, you can fix the problem by simply changing the placement of the static Marker.

This is yet another reason to put that Marker offstage, out of the user's viewing area. You can move the Marker a little to the left, or a little to the right, and edit your Movie without having to change any of the code.

Variation: Moveable Markers

In another variation of this project, you can use programmatic movement to set up three different Buttons and set the Marker to one of three positions on the screen. After the Marker is moved, the sliding Object—artwork, text, or other content—will move in relation to the Marker's new location.

View the online tutorial, and you will see that the sliding Object is parked at 55 on the x axis. I copied and pasted to create three transparent Buttons and changed the text beneath the Buttons to "Set Marker at X position and Slide."

The only code that has to be changed is to add one extra line in each of the Buttons. In the first example, the code just said, "On press, set the variable for running and make it equal to true," which triggered the code for the movement sequence. Here, I've added a piece of code for each that finds the Marker and then resets its position, depending on which Button has been pressed. You can change your code in three steps:

1. For Button 1 add these lines:

```
on (press) {
_root.marker._x = 55;
_root.running = true;
}
```

2. For Button 2 add this:

```
on (press) {
_root.marker._x = 257;
_root.running = true;
}
```

3. Finally, for Button 3 add this code:

```
on (press) {
_root.marker._x = 558;
_root.running = true;
}
```

Now, when you press a Button, the first thing the program does is set the position of the Marker. Depending on which Button is pressed next, the Marker will move to either 55, 257, or 558 on the x axis. Then it executes the movement of the sliding Object.

HOME | NEWS AND EVENTS | THE ARTISTS | FAN CLUB | PUFF DADDY PROJECTS | CONTESTS | LINKS | CONTACT

BAD BOY RECORDS

UPCOMING RELEASES

CURRENT BAD BOY
RELEASES

BAD BOY RECORDS

HOT VIDEOS

SOUNDS OFF | CLOSE WINDOW

BAD BOY ONLINE

CHECK OUT THESE OTHER BAD BOY PROJECTS

BAD BOY
ENTERTAINMENT

PUFF DADDY | NOTORIOUS BAD | FAITH EVANS | LIL' | TOTAL | BLACK ROB
CARL THOMAS | MARIO WINANS | DREAM | FUZZ & BLEU | G-DEP | MARK CURRY | THE HITMEN

PUFFY'S HOT LIST
Select an image to sample the hot list.

HOOK'T STORE

BAD BOY ONLINE

Chapter 18 - Relationships

Some years back my mom gave me a book, *Leadership in the New Science*, by Margaret J. Wheatley, which is about organization in an orderly universe. It's about chaos, fractal mathematics, and quantum mechanics. One of its concepts is that relationships can be how we observe certain forms of matter, because that's often the only way the behavior of small particles manifests itself to us.

Reading this book resulted in some of my basic thinking behind such web sites as *Barneys.com*, where a user becomes aware of the capabilities of screen Objects only by seeing a cause-and-effect relationship that's triggered by a mouse press. This is really no different from how scientists make observations in quantum mechanics: They may be able to see only the *relationship* between two things and a third thing, not any of the things themselves. But, often that's enough for them to extrapolate how those first two things are fundamentally different.

We've discussed this concept in earlier projects, such as the friction variations—the orange had a relationship with the table that it sits on, the scrollbar had a relationship with the bounding box. Relationships are integral to all forms of interactive activity.

Setting Up the Elements

In this project, we will work on and explore the relationships that can occur between two Objects. This relationship is expressed by a third Object, which is a line drawn between two squares. Moving the squares does not change the squares: Instead, it's that line that changes, in terms of not only its size but also its direction. This is a project I often teach my students, because its basic principals are integral to most work that's done in Flash. If you think about it, most interactivity involves *screen* Objects that respond to each other, acting and reacting as the movie unfolds.

Start by creating your two Objects.

1. Make a square, 20×20. (I colored mine a medium gray for the web site's online tutorial.) Name it "01 - square."

2. Our plan is to start the line at the center point of the square. So even though we've been aligning vectors at the 0 axis point, this project is a little different. Align your square center on the x axis and center on the y axis.

3. Open up the Timeline for this Movie Clip, and create a new Timeline layer called "actions." Write this code in that layer:

```
// don't use the hand icon
this.useHandCursor = false;

// handle press event
this.onPress = function() {
    this.startDrag(false, 37, 35, 702, 259);
    this.onMouseMove = function() {
        updateAfterEvent();
    };
};

// handle release event
this.onRelease = this.onReleaseOutside = function () {
    this.stopDrag();
    this.onMouseMove = undefined;
};
```

I've broken this into three blocks of code. The first removes the hand cursor, the other two handle the press and release events. The onPress is pretty self-explanatory and should be familiar to you at this point. We've set up a function, which gives the command to start dragging without locking to center and within the constraint of a rectangle that has screen coordinates of x: 25, y: 26 and x: 692, y: 249. To prevent lag time, updateAfterEvent is applied to all mouse moves, to make the square follow any dragging mouse movement at a rate that's independent of the movie's frame rate.

For onRelease and onReleaseOutside, we just want to stop dragging and nullify updateAfterEvent by undefining (thus making null) this function.

If you test your movie at this point, you should be able to drag the two squares around with your mouse.

4. Drag this Movie Clip on your Stage twice, and give them distinctive instance names:

    square_01_mc
    square_02_mc

The next phase of the project is to create the connecting line.

Designing the Relationship as an Object

Perceiving a relationship as an Object isn't so hard once you actually create it on the screen.

5. Hold down your Shift key while you select the Line tool. This will allow you to easily create a line at a 45-degree angle. Using your Info palette, make sure the line you draw has a width of 100 and a height of 100.

6. Turn this line into a new Movie Clip and name it "02 - line." Drag it onto your Stage, and give it an instance name of "line_mc."

7. Now it's time to start working in the root Timeline of this movie. Go into the root Timeline, and create a new layer called "actions." Write this code:

```
fscommand ("fullscreen", "false");
fscommand ("allowscale", "false");
stop();

// handle onEnterFrame event
_root.square_01_mc.onEnterFrame = function() {
    // scale line between square_01 and square_02
    _root.line_mc._x = this._x;
```

```
    _root.line_mc._y = this._y;
    _root.line_mc._xscale = _root.square_02_mc._x - this._x;
    _root.line_mc._yscale = _root.square_02_mc._y - this._y;
};
```

This gives directions for an onEnterFrame event and a function that will address only the instance of the first square (square _01_mc).

The first two lines of directions for say, "Go to the Stage, find the Movie Clip line_mc, and make its x and y axis positions equal to my own x and y positions." This allows the line to begin where we want it—at the center point of the first square.

The next two lines tell how and where to draw the line. We want to *scale* the size of that line between the first and second squares. The code

```
    _root.line_mc._xscale = _root.square_02_mc._x - this._x;
```

simply means "stretch the line on the x axis as far as you need to meet the center point of the second square, after you calculate the location of that second square." The next line

```
    _root.line_mc._yscale = _root.square_02_mc._y - this._y;
```

says to stretch the line on the y axis. This allows us to create a 45-degree angle line in any direction—one that's long enough to extend between the center points of both squares.

> **Note: For scaling to work, the line you drew initially must be set at 100×100. Confirm this in your Info palette. Scaling is a percentage calculation, and this makes sure you can scale up to 100 percent. A larger line, such as 120×120, would cause the line to overshoot the center point of the second square.**

Test your movie. You should see the line stretching like a rubber band any time you move either one of the two squares. This may not seem very exciting on its own, but the basic concept—turning a relationship between two Objects into a separate third Object—can be used to create some very complex interactions, including the tutorials in the next two chapters.

Chapter 19 - Using Randomness and Duplicated Movie Clips

Randomness is interesting because it can be used to execute actions that haven't been planned. As artists, we can say, "We want to be surprised." We can create a program with a certain set of boundaries, and then, perhaps, let the user, or the program itself, create a result that is unique every time it loads. We will try a simplified version of this in the chapter's project.

The first variation of the project lets the program randomly select among four Objects, which are different colored squares of the same size. In the web site's online tutorial, the colors are simply shades of gray. In the second variation, we'll be creating a simple random pattern composition on screen, using your own selection colors and shapes.

Setting Up Selections for a Simple Random Program

Before you begin coding, you need to decide which randomizing function to use. The use of the venerable random() function is deprecated these days, and math.Random(), which returns a real number rather than integers, is recommended instead. Personally, I think math.Random() is a real pain for anyone who's not a hard-core programmer. I feel the basic random() function does nearly everything you need, and oh, by the way, it's about ten times simpler. It's also the function we're using in this chapter.

When you call random(), you must then specify the number of choices the function has. For example:

```
random(4);
```

means the program will select among four random numbers.

Keep in mind, however that random() starts counting at 0. So, if you specify four possible alternatives, random() will return a choice of 0, 1, 2, and 3.

Timelines in Flash do not start at 0, however, they start at Frame 1. You'll need to do a little math to accommodate this difference when you set up the selections.

To test this out, first make yourself a Movie Clip to work with:

1. Create a Movie Clip for your Stage, and name it "01 - blocks."
2. Open the Timeline of this Movie Clip, and select its Frame 2. Draw a rectangular vector, 100×100.
3. Duplicate the vector into Frames 3, 4, and 5.

Now we have four vectors, each one in a different frame. To distinguish among them, make each one a different color. If you're following the online tutorial, Frame 2's vector is dark gray. Frame 3 is a lighter gray, Frame 4 is lighter still, and Frame 5 is white.

4. Create a new layer for this Movie Clip, and name it "actions." Put a stop() command in Frames 2,3,4, and 5:

   ```
   stop( );
   ```

5. Now, select Frame 1, and write this piece of code:

   ```
   // use of random is deprecated but still lovely
   gotoAndStop(random (4) + 2);
   ```

When we used gotoAndStop() to direct a program to a frame in earlier exercises, we would put the value or the number of that frame between the parentheses. In this case, we're putting the function random() between the parentheses of gotoAndStop().

Here, we have four frames to choose from, so you might think the correct and complete syntax would be this:

```
gotoAndStop(random(4));
```

Remember that random() starts counting at 0, and the Movie Clip has no Frame 0. We also don't want random() to include the first Frame, because the code exists in this frame. So you must add two to the number random() returns to ensure you stop at a legal frame. The correct syntax is:

```
gotoAndStop(random (4)+2);
```

By this strategy, random(0) will equal 2, which we'll use as a jump to Frame 2, where our first square exists. Random(1) will jump to Frame 3, random(2) will jump to Frame 4, and random(3) will jump to Frame 5.

This Movie Clip does not need instance names, because the code inside it is generic.

6. Drag this Movie Clip to the Stage four times.

If you test your movie at this point, the program should jump to a random frame number, choosing a different frame containing a different color rectangle every time.

Now, let's go deeper.

Drawing a Random Composition

The inspiration for this part of the tutorial comes from a book I read about the life of the American artist Jackson Pollock, who was famous for creating random compositions on a large scale. One of his statements was that he felt himself to be a painter even when the brush didn't always hit the canvas. In the same way, we can let the "machine" of a random engine create a composition on its own. In essence we program the paints, brush, canvas, strokes, rules, and boundaries. The program, however, creates the output—structuring compositions we may never have thought of.

In this project, we'll provide some predefined art, then allow the program to randomly pick some of the art and draw it on the screen.

Setting Up the Cage

We not only need to create the basic art, but also to make a place to store it. So we set up what I call a "cage" to hold the art.

1. Create a Movie Clip, and call it "02- cage." Again, go into this Movie Clip's Timeline, and name its bottom layer "vectors." In this layer, put some art into Frames 2, 3, 4, and 5. (In the online tutorial, the four abstract shapes were created by Mike Cina of **www.trueistrue.com**.) The more abstract your own shapes are, the more abstract your own composition will be.

2. Create a new layer in this Movie Clip, and name it "actions." In Frame 1 of this layer, write two lines of code:

```
stop( );
gotoAndStop(random(4)+2);
```

These directions tell the actions to first stop, then choose among a selection of four random frames. As in the previous exercise, we are directing the program to begin at Frame 2. There is no Frame 0, and Frame 1 contains the initiating code.

3. Now, let's add some more code to the actions layer. In frames 2, 3, 4, and 5 of this layer, add these lines:

```
stop ();
this._rotation = random(360);
```

The first direction, **stop ();** may seem redundant in this program, but I always put in extra stops just to be on the safe side. A screen Object can rotate 360 degrees within the flat plane of the screen, and the second line of code asks the program to pick and turn the Object, randomly, 360 degrees.

At this point we have two layers in the Timeline for the Movie Clip 02 - cage. The bottom layer, vectors, contains the four vectors. The actions layer gives the direction to randomly jump within Frames 2, 3, 4, and 5 and to select a vector there. The actions layer then gives the direction to spin the selected Object randomly, 360 degrees.

Building the Holding Pen

The second Movie Clip for this project is the action area, which I call the "holding pen."

4. Create a Movie Clip, name it "01 - holdingPen." Drag it onto your Stage, and give it an instance name of "holdingPen_mc."

5. Next, open the Movie Clip 01 - holdingPen from your Library, then place the 02- cage Movie Clip on a new layer named cage. Give it an instance name of "cage_mc."

6. Create a new layer, and name it "actions." Write this code in the layer:

```
// hide cage we are using to duplicate
this.cage_mc._visible = 0;
```

This means: "Hide the Movie Clip, make it invisible." We'll assemble the artwork onscreen by duplicating this Movie Clip, which holds our art selections. Viewers will not be able to see the master or original cage_mc Movie Clip, just the copies as they randomly appear.

Now, we will set up some initial variables that will determine how our duplicates will be placed on the screen.

7. Write this code to the actions layer:

```
// the one we are currently building
current = 0;
// the max # of cells
max = 30;
// the number of cells per row
rowSize = 10;
// the increment for each cell on the x axis
xIncrement = 60;
// the increment for each cell on the y axis
yIncrement = 60;
// set the initial offsets
xOffset = this.cage_mc._x;
yOffset = this.cage_mc._y;
```

This sequence sets the variables for the screen display. The program will begin to build the display by placing a random selection of Objects, pulled out of the cage, onto the screen. The sequence sets up some basic parameters: It tells the program to count, keep track of, and limit the total number of the Objects that are placed. It also gives the directions for how and where on the screen the Objects may be placed.

The first line simply sets up the counting, which starts at 0. The second line specifies the maximum number of Objects that can go on the screen—in this case no more than 30.

The variable rowSize places the Objects on screen in columns. The variable's value (in this example, 10) limits the number of Objects per column: three rows.

The xIncrement and yIncrement variables define the spacing within and between the columns and rows. They each have a value of 60. This means the spacing for the Objects will be 60 pixels apart on the x axis and 60 pixels apart on the y axis.

And of course we need a starting point for the first placement. The coordinates are set by the last two lines, which give the offset numbers.

Now, we could set some very firm parameters on the x and y axes for a screen starting point. But that would create a coding sequence unique to this project only. We want to create generic code, a sequence that can be used for all sorts of projects, and all sorts of Objects.

So instead of giving the offset a number, we make the offset a variable with these lines:

```
xOffset = this.cage_mc._x;
yOffset = this.cage_mc._y;
```

Our use of these variables (xOffset, yOffset) makes the offset equal to the current position derived from the answers to two questions: "Where is the cage on the x axis?" and "Where is the cage on the y-axis?"

8. Having created the offsets, finish this code sequence by adding the directions to run the action over and over:

```
this.onEnterFrame = function() {
    // make sure we aren't done
    if (current<max) {
        // determine the y # for this piece
        var y = int(current/rowSize);
        // determine the x # for this piece
        var x = current-y*rowSize;
        // duplicate this movie clip
        this.cage_mc.duplicateMovieClip("cage_mc"+current, current);
        // move it to the right x
        this["cage_mc"+current]._x = x*xIncrement+xOffset;
```

```
        // move it to the right y
        this["cage_mc"+current]._y = y*yIncrement+yOffset;
        // move on to the next cell
        ++current;
    } else {
        // place any actions here after the engine is done
    }
};
```

The first part of this code sets up what will happen if current is less than max. Remember current starts at 0, and max at 30. When current and max both equal 30, we want the program to stop.

But first, we need to describe the actions that will occur as long as current remains less than max—in other words, what will happen if there are less than 30 Objects. What we want is for the program to continue to place new Objects until that total is reached. The program will add the Objects by duplicating Movie Clips.

This only looks complicated because we are using some elements in syntax that we haven't often used before: local variables. Here, we define two local variables with the syntax **var x** and **var y**. Remember, local variables are not permanent: As soon as the if statement has finished—as soon as current equals max—then the local variables x and y will expire and go away.

Here our first local variable, x, will be equal to the integer (the nearest whole number) of current, divided by the value of rowSize. To determine y, we look at the value that will equal to current minus y, but multiplied by rowSize, in other words **(current-y)*rowSize**.

Duplicating Clips and Talking to Duplicated Clips

Once these local, temporary variables calculate, we want the program to duplicate the Movie Clip cage_mc, which contains our selection of random shapes. So we add:

```
this.cage_mc.duplicateMovieClip("cage_mc"+current, current);
```

But the duplicates of each Movie Clip must each be given a unique name. In this example, each new Movie Clip's name will be the string "cage_mc" plus the value of current. For example, on the first pass current equals 0 so the **"cage_mc"+current** will produce cage_mc0. In subsequent passes, the new Movie Clips be given individual names of cage_mc1, cage_mc2, cage_mc3, and so on.

The later part of the phrase (current) designates the depth of the Movie Clip on the z axis. This will be assigned a corresponding number, which will also be counted as 1, 2, 3, and so forth. Each new cage Movie Clip will be built above the previous level in z space.

Once we've managed to duplicate the Movie Clip, we want to move its placement upon the screen. These lines handle that direction:

```
this["cage_mc"+current]._x = x*xIncrement+xOffset;
this["cage_mc"+current]._y = y*yIncrement+yOffset;
```

To talk and give directions to duplicated Movie Clips, we must remove the period in the syntax and replace it with square brackets. This tells the program to evaluate what's inside the brackets, to look at "cage_mc" plus whatever the value of current is. When it runs for the first time, the resulting value will be:

```
this.cage_mc0._x...
```

When it runs a second time, the result will be this:

```
this.cage_mc1._x...
```

In each case, this return, which represents the location to place the next rotating shape, will be equal to the values of local variables x and y, multiplied by xIncrement and yIncrement, plus xOffset and yOffset. The next line

```
++current;
```

is the direction that tells the program to add one to current.

Again, when the program first runs, current will be equal to 0. When it runs again, current will be equal to 1. When it runs again, it will be equal to 2, and so on up to the limit of max.

The last part of the instructions concerns the else part of our if/else statement. Eventually, as the program runs, current is going to be 30, and it will equal max, and the program will stop.

Now in this example, there is nothing given for the else statement. You can feel free to place any actions here:

```
} else {
    // place any actions here after the engine is done
    }
},
```

At this point in your own work, you might proceed with a different animation or let text fade up.

If you run this movie now, you'll see a pretty fast build of 30 shapes, 3 rows, 10 in each column, and each one randomly selected and randomly rotated.

Adjusting the Speed of the Build and Completing the Project

Adjusting the speed of the build is done with your movie's frame rate. In the online tutorial, I've used a frame rate of 60 frames per second, which is really fast.

For a slower build, take the movie's frame rate down to 24 frames per second. Or use some other frame rate that suits your project.

As artists and designers we will have no control over the final execution of this animation. Within its parameters, the build is truly random, and the design is created by the program—not the user and not the artist. The engine we've created will randomly select shapes and then randomly rotate them, and no two completed screen designs will ever look the same.

I would like to see more people putting visual assets into a random engine, and then asking the engine to assemble a composition on its own. If the engine should then produce something we deem "beautiful," it could be captured and preserved by the methods described in Chapter 25, "Flash Content Beyond the Web."

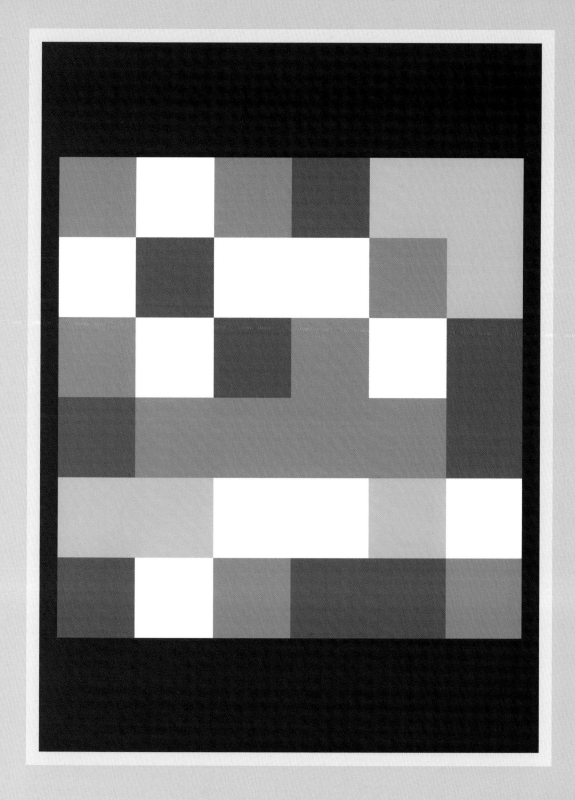

Chapter 20 - Advanced Randomness and Duplicated Clips

Now it's time to put together what you've learned so far about controlled space, relationships, and randomness.

Remember the orange on the table analogy and bounding box from Chapter 13, "Friction?" In that project, the moving Object never left the confines of the screen space defined by the bounding box. The analogy we used was an orange that bounced around on the surface of a table, but never left it.

Here, we are going to build a smarter orange: one that will notice, "Oh, I'm off the table," and, instead of falling to the ground or disappearing, will stop in mid-air, adjust its movements to jump back onto the table, and continue its random path. We will start by defining a viewable screen area with a bounding box and then create an Object that moves around randomly. Should that random movement cause it to move outside of the bounding box, a little bit of code will tell the Object to turn around and head back into viewable screen space.

Creating the Bounding Box

Before we can get the Object rolling, however, we need to set up its bounding box.

1. Using the Rectangle tool, make a rectangular vector. (The web site's online tutorial uses a width of 689 and a height of 247.) Turn this into a Movie Clip, and call it "01 - boundingBox." Place it on your Stage and give it an instance name of "boundingBox_mc."

2. This is our "table," so we want to define its boundaries, on the left, right, top, and bottom. On the root Timeline, create a new layer called "actions." Write this code there:

    ```
    fscommand ("fullscreen", "true");
    fscommand ("allowscale", "false");
    stop();
    ```

```
// get 4 coordinates of bounding box on stage
boundLeft = boundingBox_mc._x;
boundRight = boundingBox_mc._x+boundingBox_mc._width;
boundTop = boundingBox_mc._y;
boundBottom = boundingBox_mc._y+boundingBox_mc._height;
```

These four variables refer to the confines set up by our boundingBox_mc
Movie Clip. Note that we haven't merely given coordinates in hard numbers.
Here we are writing generic code; we want our boundaries to be flexible so
the code can be applied to any future project.

Build I:
Creating a Randomly Moving Object

Now that we've established where the bounding box is, how wide it is, and
how high it is, we can create the Object that will move within it.

3. Create a new layer on the root Timeline, and name it "redDot_mc." Draw
   a circle in this layer and color it red. Give it a width of 40 and a height of
   40. Press F8 to turn it into a Movie Clip. Name it "02 - redDot." Make sure
   you align this circle vector to the center inside of the Movie Clip. Return to
   the Stage, and give it an instance name of "redDot_mc."

4. Use the Align tool to align the Red Dot to the coordinates x: 50, y: 50 on
   your Stage.

5. Now let's go back into the 02 - redDot Movie Clip and write some code
   that will allow the red dot to move randomly on the Stage. Create a new
   layer in the Timeline of 02 - redDot, and name that layer "actions." Write
   these lines in the actions layer:

   ```
   // init random jumping
   randomMove = 50;
   ```

This first variable is called randomMove, and it gives the directions for a random selection.

Notice we are making randomMove equal to 50, giving it 50 (counting from 0 to 49) selections to choose from.

6. Now add the following bit of code to a function for an onEnterFrame event:

```
this.onEnterFrame = function() {
    // init Xpos movements
    newXpos = this._x+(random(randomMove)-(randomMove/2));
    curXpos = this._x;
    if (curXpos<=_root.boundLeft) {
        newXpos += random(randomMove);
    } else {
        if (curXpos>=_root.boundRight) {
            newXpos += -(random(randomMove));
        }
    }
}
```

The variable newXpos stands for "new x position," and it will be equal to where the red dot currently is on the x axis, plus the resulting value of random(randomMove) minus randomMove divided by two. What this means is, "Let me find out where I am currently on the x axis, then randomly pick a number between 0 and 49, and then subtract randomMove, divided by two. When I know the resulting number, I'll move that far on the x axis."

This math calculation allows the program to move the circle in either a positive or negative direction on the x axis. Let's say that random(randomMove) selects a value of 0. From this, we say, "subtract the value of randomMove divided by two." Remember, randomMove was given a maximum value of 50; dividing it by two returns a value of 25. The result of random(randomMove) minus 25 is –25, therefore our new x position is going to be negative 25 on the x axis.

Each time this sequence runs, newXpos (and newYpos, which you'll set up in Step 7) will create a random movement that will jump 25 pixels at a time, either left or right, up or down on the screen.

But, because this direction will continue in a loop, we always need to keep track of the starting position of the red dot. This line of code returns the variables for those numbers:

```
curXpos = this._x;
```

But we're not through yet. Having established the Object's new and current positions on the x axis, we set up an important if/else statement. The if statement:

```
if (curXpos<=_root.boundLeft) {
```

asks whether the new movement will remain within the boundary we set for x values. If the current x position is less than or equal to the variable _root.boundLeft, the new position will be outside the bounding box. In that case, we want it to move backward, in a positive direction, to get it back within the viewable area of the screen.

So whenever the if proves true, we need to set a corrective position. The next line

```
newXpos += random(randomMove);
```

handles this. Now, if the new position is too far to the left, the correction of **+= random(randomMove);** sends it back towards the right side.

Should the if statement prove false, however, that may merely mean the Object is moving right, not left. So, the subsequent else statement checks whether the Object is moving too far to the right:

```
} else {
    if (curXpos>=_root.boundRight) {
        newXpos += -(random(randomMove));
    }
}
```

If the Object has moved too far to the right, that is, if the value of curXpos is greater than the value of _root.boundRight, we need to force the new random x axis position to always be a negative number, using the calculation:

```
+=-(random(randomMove))
```

Now the random selection will go backwards, to the left, if the proposed new position is too far to the right.

The code block for newYpos is identical to that for newXpos, except it will return a value of the red dot's current location on the y axis and determine the next y axis position it should move to.

7. After the newXpos code, add the following code for the y variables. The quickest way may be simply to copy and paste the previous code block, just substituting y for x and substituting boundTop and boundBottom for boundLeft and boundRight.

```
// init Ypos movements
newYpos = this._y+(random(randomMove)-randomMove/2);
curYpos = this._y;
if (curYpos<=_root.boundTop) {
    newYpos += random(randomMove);
} else {
    if (curYpos>=_root.boundBottom) {
        newYpos += -(random(randomMove));
    }
}
```

The program now checks to see if the top and bottom boundaries are being respected. If all is in order, the next screen position of the red dot (newXpos, newYpos) will be allowed.

8. Finally, you need to send the red dot to its new x and y positions. Add these final lines after the Ypos sequence:

```
// execute movement
this._x = newXpos;
this._y = newYpos;
};
```

The red dot now will take a 25-pixel jump in a direction that is completely random. If you run your movie, you should see the red dot moving randomly around the screen, always returning to the viewable area if it drifts away.

At this point, save your work and use Save As to make a new file. You'll be needing it.

Build II:
Introducing a Second Object

Working on the foundation of the previous exercise, we'll add a second Object to join the red dot in its travels.

1. To get the second Object onto the screen, open up your Library and duplicate your 02 - redDot Movie Clip. Name this new duplicated clip "03 - greenDot."
2. Open up this Movie Clip and its circle layer and highlight the vector there. Change the color of the circle from red to green.
3. Go back into the root Timeline, and create a new layer named "greenDot" above the redDot layer. Drag the 03 - greenDot Movie Clip out onto your Stage. Give it an instance name of "greenDot_mc," and place this Movie Clip on coordinates of x: 50, y: 100, which is just below the redDot_mc Movie Clip.

The movement code is already inside this duplicated clip. If you test your movie at this point, you should see two dots, one red and one green, moving about randomly.

Save your work, using Save As to make a new file, and we'll move ahead.

Build III:
Adding a Connecting Line

As we did in Chapter 18's relationships project, here we'll add a connecting line between the two moving dots. This adds a third element to the screen display, one that will vary depending on where the dots are traveling.

1. If you've already completed the project given in Chapter 18, the shortcut way to do this is to simply copy the Line Movie Clip you created for the relationships tutorial and rename the Library name "04 - line" for this project.

   Note: If you haven't completed the Chapter 18 tutorial, you'll need to create the line for this project. Use the Line tool to make a line from the top left to the bottom right at a 45-degree angle. (Any time you hold down the Shift key while using the Line tool, you'll always draw a line in degree increments of 45). In the Info palette, make sure the line has a width of 100 and a height of 100, so the line will scale properly. Turn this into a Movie Clip and name it 04 - line.

2. Go back to the Stage, create a new layer of the root Timeline, and call that layer "line." Drag out the Movie Clip 04 - line, and position it *offscreen*. Give it an instance name of "line_mc."

3. At this point we want to make an amendment to the code of the red dot's Movie Clip. So open up the Timeline for 02 - redDot, and highlight its actions layer. We're going to add a new block of code to the onEnterFrame directions, so write this code below what is there:

```
// scale line between the red dot and the green dot
    _root.line_mc._x = this._x;
    _root.line_mc._y = this._y;
    _root.line_mc._xscale = _root.greenDot_mc._x-this._x;
    _root.line_mc._yscale = _root.greenDot_mc._y-this._y;
};
```

This coding says, "Go to the stage, find the Line, set its x and y positions with the red dot's x and y locations, and then scale a line between this and the current x and y location of the green dot." This creates the line between the red and green dots, even as the dots are moving.

If you run your movie at this point, you should see a line being drawn and scaling proportionately, between the moving positions of the red dot and the green dot.

Save this, and then make a new file with Save As so we can move forward again.

Build IV:
Duplicating Movie Clips

This project builds upon the last exercise and will let the program create random line drawings as it runs.

At present, the line redraws itself proportionately between both dots. In this version, we'll duplicate this Line Movie Clip and allow the copies of the line to remain on the screen as the program runs.

1. The first thing we'll do make a small change to the code in the actions layer of the red dot's Movie Clip. We're going to ask the program to do some counting, so we'll add a new variable, called "lineNum." Standing for "line number," lineNum will start counting at 1. Adjust your code as shown in the highlighting:

    ```
    // init random jumping
    randomMove = 50;

    // start a variable to count our duplicated movie clips
    lineNum = 1;
    ```

2. Next, we need to make a few changes to the onEnterFrame directions for the red dot. Remove this code:

```
// scale line between redDot and the greenDot
_root.line_mc._x = this._x;
_root.line_mc._y = this._y;
_root.line_mc._xscale = _root.greenDot_mc._x-this._x;
_root.line_mc._yscale = _root.greenDot_mc._y-this._y;
};
```

and replace it with the code that is highlighted below:

```
//duplicate line between redDot and the greenDot
_parent.line_mc.duplicateMovieClip ("newLine_mc" + lineNum, lineNum);

_parent["newLine_mc" + lineNum]._x = this._x;
_parent["newLine_mc" + lineNum]._y = this._y;

_parent["newLine_mc" + lineNum]._xscale = _parent.greenDot_mc._x-this._x;
_parent["newLine_mc" + lineNum]._yscale = _parent.greenDot_mc._y-this._y;

lineNum++;
};
```

Notice we don't want to just scale the line anymore. We want to make a copy of it, and then let the copy of the line remain on screen. So we say:

```
_parent.line_mc.duplicateMovieClip ("newLine_mc" + lineNum, lineNum);
```

That means "Go up one, find the Movie Clip named line_mc, and make a duplicate of it."

Note that we still want to scale the line; we just don't want to scale the *same* line each time. Each new duplicated Movie Clip will draw a line that's different in length and in direction, and all the different lines remain in view.

I like animations to look crisp, so let's add a finishing touch.

3. Go back into the root Timeline of this movie, and in the actions layer, write the following highlighted code:

```
fscommand ("fullscreen", "false");
fscommand ("allowscale", "false");
stop();
    // bump quality down to low
    _root._highquality = false;
```

This means "make this movie the default low quality."

Now, when you run the movie, the fuzziness of the lines has disappeared, and crisp, hard lines appear between the two moving dots.

Run this movie for a while, and you'll notice that the dots slow down. That's because every time you duplicate a Movie Clip, you duplicate something that has its own independent Timeline. Each time you do this, you take a little tiny nibble out of memory. When you keep nibbling on memory, there eventually won't be much memory left and your system will slow.

On a conceptual level, you might think of duplicating Movie Clips as a process that's like birth. Each duplicate is born and lives its life on the Stage. And they never die. The whole society that you've created on the Stage does start to get crowded, and things start breaking down.

To make this society happier, we have to implement death. We need a way to remove or destroy the newly born Movie Clips after they have lived their useful lifespan—a way to make room for the later generations of duplicated Movie Clips that have yet to be born. This way we give back memory to the program, sustaining the activity at least until the viewer tires of the game.

Save your file, and do a Save As to start a new file that will deal with this issue.

Build V:
Implementing Death

To fix this, we need to make a small adjustment in the Movie Clip 04 - line.

1. Open the Timeline of 04 - line, and expand its Timeline to a span of 50 frames.

2. Create a new layer in this Timeline, and name it "actions." In frame 50 of this layer, write these two lines:

```
stop();
this.removeMovieClip();
```

This is all we need to do to make each line "live" for the lifespan of 50 frames, and then die and remove itself.

Now if you test your movie, you'll see the file never slows down, and the earlier lines that were drawn soon disappear.

Save this file, and do a Save As to create a new file for the final version of this project.

Build VI:
An Abstract Composition

When I was working on this project, what I thought was most interesting was the relationship between the red dot and the green dot, and how the distance between them was expressed.

I wasn't so much interested in the dots, though. So, why not hide them?

All we need to do is add one small snippet of code to hide the red dot and the green dot.

1. Go into the Movie Clip 02 - redDot, and add this highlighted bit of code at the very top of its instructions:

```
//turn object's visibility off
this._visible = false;
randomMove = 50;
lineNum = 1;
```

2. Copy this, and do the same for the Movie Clip 03 - greenDot:

```
this._visible = false;
randomMove = 50;
```

Now when you run your Movie, the dots are hidden, but lines are still being drawn to stretch the distance between the dots. The program is still calculating where the Dots are, even though the dots have been hidden from view. The program continues to execute the duplication of the movie clips that form the lines. It will form an abstract composition, and the viewer can't see how it's being done.

Because the line the engine is duplicating is a Movie Clip, I hope you realize that you could use any other type of artwork in place of a line. The illustrations at the end of this chapter show you some of the possibilities of this engine. The first two illustrations use drawn lines to create their compositions, the third, "Lightning Architecture," employs jagged abstract shapes, and the fourth, "Bacteria," uses circles. They illustrate four entirely different styles, but all use this same engine.

Chapter 21 - Transfer of Power

This last tutorial is probably the most advanced—but not in terms of its concepts. As we have throughout this book, again we will combine small ideas to create something more complex.

Here, the ideas combine to give you a strategy for deploying several functions within the same movie. Specifically, two engines—a moving scrollbar and a set of Buttons—will be able to control the same set of Objects on your Stage. Although both can control the content in this project, they can't control it at the same time. If they did, the program would be fighting itself internally.

When we give each controller a means to turn itself on, we'll write a program that, in effect, can "turn off" the other controller. Actually the program will transfer the power to control content from one Object to the other Object— even while the user is in the middle of using one or the other to manipulate what's seen on screen.

This is similar to the system I used for Motown.com (**www.motown.com**, click on Classic Motown). This part of the web site is a chronological display of music-related content, divided into a historic Timeline by significant dates. The various sections of this moveable display can be viewed when the user activates one of two controlling devices. You can manipulate the scrollbar, or you can click on a navigation button assigned to a particular date on the timeline, such as 1962.

So, two engines—the navigation buttons at the top of the screen and the scrollbar at the bottom—can affect one piece of content in the middle of the screen.

Note: Classic Motown was originally built in Flash 4, so the version of the file used in the online tutorial has been updated to Flash MX.

Classic Motown.

Tip: I keep a template file for elements that I'm always using, such as the transparent Button, so I don't have to recreate them over and over again. On my desktop, I keep a file called template.fla. This file contains a transparent Button. The actions layer in its Timeline already has a series of typical FS Commands and stops in the first frame.

Setting Up the Scrollbar Engine

We'll start with a concept we've already created: Chapter 13's Friction project has a scrollbar that can be adapted for this project. That basic Friction project, however, had all its code inside of the scrollbar. Because we're adding a second engine here, it's better if we write most the code on the root Timeline.

To keep track of all elements, you should first create two folders in your Library. Name them "01 - Scrollbar Assets" and "02 - Timeline Assets."

1. Go into your Library, create a new Movie Clip, and call it "01 - ScrollbarGutter." Take the Rectangle tool, turn Line off, and do a solid fill with a width of 687 and a height of 14.

2. Create a new layer of the root Timeline and call it scrollbarGutter. Drag out 01 - ScrollbarGutter to your Stage and onto that layer. Align the gutter to the bottom left, to coordinates of x: 26 and y: 256. It will look like a thin strip across the bottom of your Stage. Give it an instance name of "scrollbarGutter_mc."

3. Now it's time to create the scrollbar itself. Go into the Library, create a new Movie Clip and call it "02 - scrollbar." This will be created as rectangle with a width of 100 and a height of 12.

4. Go into the root Timeline, create a new layer, and name it "scrollbar." Drag the Movie Clip of the scrollbar onto your Stage and align it at x: 34, y: 248. Give it an instance name of "scrollbar_mc."

We've got one interface down, and one to go.

Building the Buttons

It's time to make the buttons.

5. Create a new layer on the root Timeline, and name it "topnav text."

6. Use the Text tool to name a series of Buttons. However, you don't have to create four different pieces of text, just one. Just use Static Text to write the words **Section 01**, **Section 02**, **Section 03**, and **Section 04** as a single line of text, with some spaces between to spread them out across the screen.

7. Now create another new layer on the root Timeline, and name that layer "topnav buttons." Drag out four transparent Buttons from your Library onto your Stage or create them from scratch (See Chapter 7, "Movie Clips as Buttons and the One Button Trick"). Resize them all to a width of 70 and a height of 20. Place each of the Buttons over the text so that Section 01 has its own Button, Section 02 has its own, and so on.

At this point we have elements for two engines, but we haven't written any code yet.

Setting Up Some Content

The next step is to create the Movie Clip in which the content will reside and which the two engines will attempt to control.

8. Go into the Library, and create a new Movie Clip. Name this Movie Clip "01 - content." This will be an empty Movie Clip, with nothing in it.

9. Go back to your Stage, and at the very bottom layer on your root Timeline, create and name a layer "content_mc." Drag the Movie Clip 01 - content into this layer and position it at x: 26; y: 54. This should place it just underneath the text and buttons for the topnav navigation bar. Give it an instance name of "content_mc."

10. Having created and placed an empty Movie Clip that will load and hold sections of content, we can go ahead and create some content for those sections. Go back into the Library, create a new Movie Clip, and name it "02 - section." Create this as a rectangular vector, with a width of 687 and a height of 187.

We'll be writing some code that will talk to section_mc and duplicate it inside of content_mc. But, we need to link it in order to use it.

11. Right-click on the Movie Clip 02 - section to open the contextual sub-menu choices. Select the one called Linkage.

12. Under Linkage, check Export For ActionScript and Export in First Frame.

The program will ask you to give an *identifier*. Identifiers are a bit like instance names; they are unique to individual Objects. For this project, write in the name "section" as the identifier.

Writing the Code

Now that all the elements have been established, we can start writing the code that will control them all. There are actually eight parts to this code, so we will handle them one at a time.

13. Create a new layer on the root Timeline and name it "actions." Write this code in first:

```
//on root Timeline :
fscommand ("fullscreen", "false");
fscommand ("allowscale", "false");
stop ();
```

14. Our next block of code deals with the gutter and how the scrollbar will move in it. Add the lines:

```
// set up gutter info
gutterLeft = scrollbarGutter_mc._x+1;
gutterRight = scrollbarGutter_mc._x + (scrollbarGutter_mc._width -
_root.scrollbar_mc._width) - 1;
```

Here, we're moving left or right only, and we're adding a one-pixel increment on both sides as a visual cushion. The variable gutterLeft will be equal to the gutter's location on the x axis, plus one pixel. The variable gutterRight takes into account this location but first subtracts the size of the scrollbar from its own length before subtracting the last pixel. (For a refresher on this, see Chapter 13, "Friction.")

The next phase of the project deals with loading the content onto the screen in a specific arrangement. To do this, we'll create an *array*.

Setting Up an Array

An *array* is a wonderful piece of useful code. I like to think of it as something of a grocery list. At home, my wife's grocery lists are written on a lined pad. Each line has a different item on it: bread, milk, apples, and so on. These items represent data, and all refer to something I'm supposed to go out and get. In Flash, an array is also arranged as a series of lines with items on each line. The items can be something you are telling the program to go out and get, as well.

One minor difference between an array and my wife's grocery lists is that in Flash, the first item in an array is numbered 0. The next items are numbered 1, 2, 3, and so on.

15. To begin, we only need to name the array and tell how big it is. To do so, add this code:

```
// create an array for attaching new sections on our Timeline
section = new Array(4);
max = _root.section.length;
itemDepth = 1;
```

The first line names the array as "section" and sets up how many items are in this "grocery list." Here there are four items (0, 1, 2, 3).

The second line sets a variable called "max," which will be equal to how long the array section is. In this case, max should return the value of 4.

We'll be laying the sections of content down, end on end, in separate layers in this movie. To do this stacking, we need to let the program know there will be some levels of depth and to tell it to do some counting so it can keep track of the levels. So here the variable itemDepth will be set to 1.

16. The directions to lay down the content end to end are a bit trickier:

```
// how and where to attach new sections
for (i=0; i<max; i++) {
// attach new item
_root.content_mc.attachMovie("section", "section_"+i, itemDepth);
curItem = content_mc["section_"+i];
// put the MC in an array
_root.section[i] = curItem;
if (i == 0) {
curItem._x = 0;
} else {
curItem._x = content_mc._width+1;
}
itemDepth++;
}
```

What we're creating here is called a *for loop*. No, we haven't used this before. Previously, we've asked programs to execute something once or run something continuously. A for loop is another way to tell a program to repeat a command, but only for a specific number of times.

Using the For Loop

Let's go through the for loop one line at a time. The first line

```
for (i=0; i<max; i++) {
```

tells the program to keep running as long as i is less than max, which equals 4. The **i ++** means, "each time this runs, increment the value of i after each iteration of the for loop." This for loop will run the subsequent set of actions only four times, or until i becomes greater than max, then it will quit.

The next lines start attaching the sections and sew them together. The snippet

```
// attach new item
_root.content_mc.attachMovie("section", "section_"+i, itemDepth);
curItem = content_mc["section_"+i];
```

says, "Please go to the Stage, go into the empty Movie Clip called content_mc, and attach our linked movie."

These directions tell the program what the name of the Movie Clip is that we want to attach. To start, we named it section. We're going to have to give it a new instance name each time, so we'll name the first one "section_+i," which also tells the program to start incrementing. This will give each loaded section a unique instance name, which will be "section_0" the first time, "section_1" the second time, "section_2" the third time, and "section_3" the fourth and last time.

By choosing and using depths, each section will also arrive on a slightly different depth on the Stage. The next lines set up a new variable, curItem, which indicates the path where the attached Movie Clips can be found. This is essential in order to be able to address these clips at any time.

These lines place each newly attached section into an array, and give directions where they should be positioned on screen:

```
// put the MC in an array
_root.section[i] = curItem;
if (i == 0) {
curItem._x = 0;
} else {
curItem._x = content_mc._width+1;
}
itemDepth++;
}
```

The first line gives the direction to set up an array called section that will be equal to curItem. In other words, it's building a new grocery list, and each line in the grocery list is the path that indicates where to find these newly attached sections. Once we have constructed an array that contains a path to each section, we now want to give directions for the positioning of each section on the screen.

This is done as the if/else statement

```
if (i == 0) {
  curItem._x = 0;
  } else {
  curItem._x = content_mc._width+1;
  }
```

that says, "If i is found to be equal to 0 (in other words, when this runs for the first time), please place the first item at the x-axis location of 0."

When the next iteration of the loop runs, the if portion fails, and the program turns to the else portion, which says "Make the x axis position of the next item equal to the first item's width, plus one." This attaches the second item right after the first with a one-pixel buffer in between. As it continues to attach items, it will always check to see how much of the x axis has already been taken, so it can lay down the next item in the right place. We also need keep track of the depth as they're stacking, so we need this line:

```
itemDepth++;
```

Once each section arrives on the Stage with a unique instance name and its own depth and it is laid down in the proper order, the section can be accessed and further manipulated by the buttons and the scrollbar we created earlier on.

If you test your movie at this point, it should grab sections and lay them down, arranging them end to end, from left to right.

Defining Movements of the Content

After we load the content, we need to measure it for scrolling purposes. Next, we must define the scrolling function.

17. To set up two new variables that define the movement boundaries, add these lines:

```
// set the info about the content
contentRight = content_mc._x;
contentLeft = 712 - content_mc._width;
```

The first variable, contentRight, tells us how far right the content sections will be able to move. Similarly, contentLeft tells us how far left the content sections will be able to move, and here the value 712 represents the size of the viewable area of the screen. (This number will vary depending upon the size of the viewable area in your own projects.) By subtracting the total width of the content from 712, we obtain a final reading on how far left the content can move.

18. The next block of code handles the function that will define the scrolling of the content. Add these lines:

```
// calculate the current percentage of the scrollbar
function scrollBarFunc() {
  var percent = (scrollbar_mc._x-gutterLeft)/(gutterRight-gutterLeft);
  content_mc._x = percent*(contentLeft-contentRight)+contentRight;
  updateAfterEvent();
}
```

The function's name, scrollBarFunc, is short for "scrollbar function." The first line of the function sets up a local variable, percent, which will be equal to the percentage the scrollbar can move, in relation to the size of its gutter. In the next line, the resulting percentage is used to direct the movement of the content Movie Clip. Their movement will be in the same percentage proportion to the movements of the scrollbar, but within their own left and right parameters and in the opposite direction. (For a more detailed explanation of percentage mapping, see Chapter 14, "Friction Variations.")

Transferring Power

The fifth block of code sets up two functions that allow the topNav elements to control the scrolling movements. Here is where the transfer of power begins: The topNav buttons will not control the content directly but instead will tell the scrollbar to move, and then the scrollbar will move the content.

19. Add these directions for the transfer:

```
// jump the scrollbar to an area on the gutter that equals the beginning of each section
function contentFunc() {
// is the difference between the goal and the position small?
if (Math.abs(scrollBarGoal-scrollbar_mc._x)<1 || !topNav) {
// if so, position  everything  where it needs to be and stop
scrollbar_mc._x = scrollBarGoal;
content_mc._x = contentGoal;

// transfer power  by turning  scrollbar  actions off
onEnterFrame = null;

} else {
// otherwise  move scrollbar  and adjust content
scrollbar_mc._x += (scrollbarGoal-scrollbar_mc._x)/6;
scrollBarFunc();
}
}

function moveContent(s) {
// transfer power - turn topNav actions on
topNav = true;
// where should the content go
contentGoal = contentRight - section[s]._x;
// make sure it's not off the screen!
if (contentGoal<contentLeft) {
contentGoal = contentLeft;
}
```

```
// what percent is that goal?
var percent = -(contentGoal-contentRight)/((contentRight-contentLeft));
// apply that percent to the gutter size to determine the scrollbar's goal
scrollbarGoal = percent*(gutterRight-gutterLeft)+gutterLeft;
// set up a loop to move the content and scrollbar
onEnterFrame = contentFunc;
}
```

We need to set up two functions for this. The first is called contentFunc, and it involves setting up a goal, evaluating how close we are to the goal, and moving to the goal. (These "goals" are defined as the variables scrollbarGoal and contentGoal.)

So, we set up an if/else statement that uses Math.abs to look and see if the scrollbar's position is either plus or minus one pixel of a determined goal on the x axis.

If the scrollbar is within one pixel, it will snap to a goal point and stop there. The content Movie Clip, which the scrollbar is controlling, will snap to its own goal point and stop.

But there's still a lot of complex activity going on. If the scrollbar is not within one pixel of any goal, the default of the else tells the scrollbar to keep moving until it does come within one pixel of a goal. This part of the directions asks "Where am I? Where is my goal? How far is the distance? What is the speed of my movement to get there?" (See Chapter 17, "Programmatic Movement," for a more thorough discussion of this calculation for difference and speed.)

The last line of this section

```
scrollBarFunc();
```

tells the program to go ahead and run the function called scrollBarFunc. Remember, we've already set up the function scrollBarFunc to move the content in relation to the movement of the scrollbar. (See Step 18.) This completes the hand-off. The buttons are now controlling the scrollbar, and the scrollbar is moving the content.

Note that the first function of the topNav, contentFunc, looks at goals and whether the scrollbar and content are near their goals, but we haven't really set our goals.

Well, goal setting is going to be part of the function called moveContent. The syntax is:

```
function moveContent(s) {
```

That little "s" is a variable that is passed to the function moveContent. In effect, any button presses on the topNav will be passing along the data of the argument represented by "s." This data will be a number that correlates to a desired section movement.

But our first direction for this function is a transfer of power. The line

```
topNav = true;
```

turns on the topNav buttons by making a variable topNav equal to true.

The rest of this code block defines the goals for the moving content and the moving scrollbar. Here, contentGoal equals its farthest right side location, minus **section(s)_x**. Remember, s is a value that we're going to be passing in, which will let us know whether we'll be talking to either Section0, Section1, Section2, or Section3.

We also need to make sure the movement doesn't go off the screen, so we say, "If contentGoal is less than contentLeft, just move it to the position of contentLeft." These lines help keep the content on the screen:

```
// make sure it's not off the screen!
if (contentGoal<contentLeft) {
 contentGoal = contentLeft;
}
```

We must remember also that all the movements will be mapped as a percentage. The lines

```
var percent = -(contentGoal-contentRight)/((contentRight-contentLeft));
scrollbarGoal = percent*(gutterRight-gutterLeft)+gutterLeft;
```

look up the current value of the local variable percent and apply that percentage to the scrollbar's goal to determine the movement.

The last line sets up an onEnterFrame to start the loop and run the function contentFunc over and over again:

```
// set up a loop to move the content and scrollbar
 onEnterFrame = contentFunc;
}
```

This completes the movement of the content.

Final Instructions for the Scrollbar and Buttons

The last three sections of code define the press and release of the lower scrollbar so it too can scroll the contents, and they define an onEnterFrame method with a few more variables that provide a bit of "friction" for this as well.

20. Add this code to the actions layer of the root Timeline:

```
// don't use the hand icon
scrollbar_mc.useHandCursor = false;
```

21. Add this code as well:

```
// handle press event
scrollbar_mc.onPress = function() {
this.startDrag(false, _root.gutterLeft, this._y, _root.gutterRight, this._y);
// transfer power - turn topNav actions off
topNav = false;
dragging = true;
this.onMouseMove = function() {
_root.scrollBarFunc();
updateAfterEvent();
};
};

// handle release event
scrollbar_mc.onRelease = scrollbar_mc.onReleaseOutside = function() {
this.onMouseMove = undefined;
this.stopDrag();
dragging = false;
xSpeed = (newxpos-oldxpos)*RATIO;
};
// set initial variables
FRICTION = .9;
RATIO = .5;
dragging = false;

// handle onEnterFrame event
scrollbar_mc.onEnterFrame = function() {
if (!dragging && !topNav) {
oldxpos = this._x;
newxpos = oldxpos+xSpeed;
xSpeed *= FRICTION;
if (newxpos>gutterRight || newxpos<gutterLeft) {
xSpeed *= -FRICTION;
newxpos = oldxpos;
}
this._x = newxpos;
_root.scrollBarFunc();
} else {
oldxpos = newxpos;
newxpos = this._x;
}
};
```

Here we're asking that the onPress execute certain actions and then, a specific function, when the user presses upon the scrollbar's Movie Clip. The instructions include defining the limits of where the scrollbar may be dragged (the limits of its gutter) and telling the program to "turn off" the topNav Buttons. This is accomplished by making the variable topNav equal false. We give the go-ahead for dragging by making dragging equal to true.

At this point, things may be making a bit more sense. You now can see that when a user presses the scrollbar, the program will turn the topNav actions off, so that only the scrollbar can move the content, and then we tell the program to go ahead and execute the function scrollBarFunc whenever the mouse is moved. This will allow the scrollbar—and only the scrollbar— to control the content.

What happens when a user lets go of the scrollbar? Well, we don't necessarily want to turn topNav on immediately. The user may start doing something else instead. So our first direction is to make onMouseMove equal to undefined. This tells the program to stop the updateAfterEvent because we don't need it anymore. At the same time, we'll set dragging equal to false.

We do want the user to be aware that control of the scrollbar has been relinquished. So, we'll use a gentle, gliding friction movement of the scrollbar to let it slow down and stop. To handle the friction aspects of the onRelease event, we'll set up the initial variables of RATIO and speed, as we've done in several other tutorials. (See Chapter 13, "Friction," if you need a refresher.) The only difference in this code is that the onEnterFrame refers specifically to the scrollbar, like this:

```
scrollbar_mc.onEnterFrame = function() {
```

You'll also notice that there's a small adjustment to the if/else statement. Instead of just noting whether or not the program is not dragging, we're also asking it to make sure that the topNav is not activated either, like this:

```
if (!dragging && !topNav) {
```

The rest of the computation for friction should be familiar, except we ask that the program also run the function for scrollBarFunc. This assures that as the scrollbar is slowing down to a stop the functions it had been given—meaning control of the content—will also have friction applied. Now the content will slow down with a friction effect as well.

The else kicks in if the scrollbar is being pressed again.

At this point, you can test your Movie. Everything should work fabulously, except for those topNav Buttons. The array should build out on the screen, and pressing the scrollbar should move these content sections right or left, in reverse direction to how the scrollbar is moved.

To activate the Buttons, we just need a small adjustment to their onPress, which will pass on the argument found within "s."

21. Add the following code to the onPress directions for *each* of the four Transparent Buttons. For Button 1, add this:

```
on (press) {
 moveContent(0);
}
```

For Button 2, add this:

```
on (press) {
 moveContent(1);
}
```

For Button 3, add this:

```
on (press) {
 moveContent(2);
}
```

For Button 4, add this:

```
on (press) {
 moveContent(3);
}
```

These four additions supply the information for s and move the content to any of the predetermined goals. (When the user presses any button, the program will call the function moveContent, which we defined earlier in Step 17.) It will supply the individual name of each of the content Movie Clips that had been loaded into the section Movie Clip, which had been assigned numbers during the loading process (section_0, section_1, and so on).

Now, if you test your movie and press any button, the buttons will control the content in a slightly different way than the scrollbar did. Instead of a smooth glide that mimics the mouse pressing on the scrollbar, a press of a button will shuttle the sections so that the user may arrive at the starting point of any of the four sections.

You'll notice that the scrollbar moves as well. This illustrates how this transfer of power is a three-tier, three-step process:

1. The user presses any NavBar button.
2. The button activates the scrollbar.
3. The scrollbar activates the moving content.

When the scrollbar is being used, the buttons relinquish their power until one of them is pressed.

Some Final Thoughts

The goal of this technique should be an intuitive manipulation of screen Objects that can be switched back and forth from one form of user interface to another. All elements can play together harmoniously and seamlessly.

Additional sections of content may be added, or the content may be updated. This generic code for transfer of power needs no further adjustments and will continue to provide all the calculations required for proportional movements.

This is the final tutorial, and I'd like to say that I could not have been able to complete it without the help of colleague Branden Hall.

I went to art school, I'm no mathlete. Branden has really helped me with the math concepts that have helped to make the code of this particular project so generic and transparent. It seems fitting, then, to end this portion of the book with a few words from Branden on the subject of writing elegant code.

Chapter 22 - Writing Elegant Code

by Branden Hall

Because you have read this far, your head is probably swimming with ideas. I think you'll agree that Josh has a gift for teaching complex ideas in a very approachable and exciting way. His ability to teach in such an engaging way, I think, stems from the way he learns. He explores. He pokes. He prods. Most of all though, he plays.

It's this kind of playfulness that I believe drives the success of many people in the world of web development. In fact, all of the web development all-stars that I have met share this attribute: They are all simply excited by learning new things. To be honest, I don't think that you can be very successful in any creative field if you don't love to learn.

Code and Art

This brings up a particular point when it comes to web development: The line between programmers and artists. When the web was young, programmers wore all of the hats and did the design (if you could call it that) as well as the coding. Then, with the rise of the concept of table-based layout, visual artists started joining the party. For the most part though, their role was limited to the digital version of brochure layout.

In web development, applications and programming languages are your palette and brush. Think about it: You will rarely, if ever, meet a "traditional" artist who only knows how to create in a single medium. They may specialize in a particular medium, but they are by no means limited to it.

In recent years we've started to see more artists delving into the realm of programming, particularly with Java and Flash. There still aren't a lot of artists, however, who have sat down and learned how to write code well. And this, I feel, is a great shame.

Most artists I know are content to learn just enough code to do what they need to do and then hastily run back to Photoshop. I think part of the reason is that code reminds people too much of math, something that many artists don't particularly care for. What most people fail to grasp is that code is just another type of brush. And just as you can use a brush to simply coat a wall in paint or to transform it into a mural, you can use code in a minimal, utilitarian manner or you can use it to create works of art.

Remember too that, as with painting, there are always new techniques to learn when it comes to coding. By learning and practicing programming, your code will become both more functional and more elegant. As an artist, elegance of code is something worth striving for.

Elegance Through Simplicity

Since ancient times, mathematicians have spoken of particular mathematical solutions being "elegant." You will quite often hear the term applied to engineering also. In both cases, elegant usually means simple, yet amazingly robust, to the point of giving the equation or machine a particular type of beauty.

It was, in fact, that type of beauty that got me interested in engineering and programming. I first discovered it in a toy train I had as a child. This train was, for lack of a better term, *cool*. You wound it up, and it chugged across the floor playing the pre-kindergarten hit "This Old Man" as it went. This by itself was pretty neat, because in those days computer chips had not yet made their way into toys. But there was more: The train's shell was made out of clear plastic, and each one of the gears, springs, miniature bellows, and whistles working inside was brightly colored. It was so elegant! You could see exactly what it was doing, yet comprehending how those few parts combined do such a cool thing was difficult to say the least. It was plain and simply awe-inspiring.

This is the same kind of elegant beauty that code can have. There's a practical benefit too: Simple, elegant code tends to run better and have fewer bugs than complex code. This means that you can, plain and simply, do more when you write beautiful code.

By striving to write such code, you will force yourself to learn more about programming, and that constant struggle to learn more is one of the keys to becoming a great programmer—and a great artist.

Part III - Into the Real World

Chapter 23 - Relationships Between Flash and HTML

Flash is an Internet technology that can be delivered entirely over the web. Once the plug-in "player" software has been downloaded successfully by a user, your Flash movies can be downloaded and viewed—by a potentially vast audience.

But before this can happen, you need to embed, or place, your Flash movie in a program format that's readable by the user's browser. The format and language most often used today is the decade-old hypertext markup language, HTML.

There are two *tags* you must write to embed your movie into HTML. One is called the OBJECT tag, and the other is the EMBED tag.

The OBJECT tag is read by Microsoft's Internet Explorer (IE) browser. The EMBED tag is read by Netscape's browser. You really need to write the tags for both of these two common browser systems.

Why? When Explorer comes across an EMBED tag, it says, "Oh, I don't know what this is," and will skip everything that's been placed within that tag. When it comes to an OBJECT tag, it says, "Oh, I know what this is," and will then play your movie. And when Netscape's browser comes across an OBJECT tag, it will ignore it or skip it; it will recognize only an EMBED tag.

Writing the OBJECT and EMBED Tags

There are a number of elements, called *parameters*, which are selectable when writing an OBJECT tag for the Explorer browser.

The first is the Class ID, which defines the code as an OBJECT tag for Flash. Next, the code base allows you to tag your project with a number that corresponds to the version of code you wrote in. If you're working in Flash MX, for example, your version name should start with the number 6.

In many cases, the user's browser will recognize the version and make adjustments or updates to the user's computer. For example, the current version of Explorer running on a PC will read this part of the tag, and if the user has a version of Flash that is older than what you've embedded, it will automatically install the player software for the new version.

Another selectable parameter is quality. This refers to the resolution of the image on screen. Flash lets you select different levels of quality: low, medium, and high. (Flash 4 only let you choose between low and high.)

Why, for example, would you ever choose low quality? Low is obviously going to chew up your type fonts, and the graphics will look ragged or rough. But low is going to run really, really fast. High will give a smooth, anti-aliased look to all your artwork, but if you have anything heavily interactive going on, it will run very slow. This can be a problem for users and web site visitors who are running systems with older CPUs that have less processing power.

For the parameter, play, you can select either True or False. You might select True if you have an opening animation sequence and want the playhead to start playing that Timeline automatically. But you might choose False if your movie involved some programmatic interactions. In this case, the first frame would not begin to play any of these animations but merely present elements the user might manipulate.

For the parameter, loop, I suggest selecting False. I usually don't want the movie to loop because I want to control this functionality of the movie on my end with ActionScript.

For the parameter name, menu, I also pick False. Leaving the default of True means that if a user right-clicks (or Ctrl-clicks for Mac) on your movie, a contextual menu will appear, allowing the user to do things like zoom in or zoom out, restart an animation, or view it at 100% of screen.

Now on some sites, there may be some merit to adding this extra level of interactivity and permitting the user to zoom in or restart animations at will. But for me, what the user should see should, ideally, be consistent with what I or the client want the user to see. If the point of your movie is to get a message across, it's best to disable this user option. Most people never use these features anyway, so it doesn't hurt to make this parameter False.

Background color, or bgcolor, is another parameter. What is the background of the movie going to be? Sometimes I don't need to fill my entire movie space with vectors, so I need a background color. Generally, I choose the same color that is the background color in the body of my HTML. This makes things visually consistent, smooth, and flush.

Here is an example of HTML coding; the OBJECT tag appears first, followed by the EMBED tag:

```
<html>
<head>
<title>PrayStation</title>
</head>

<body bgcolor="#242424" marginwidth="0" marginheight="0" topmargin="0"
leftmargin="0">

<table width="100%" height="100%" cellpadding="0" cellspacing="0" border="0">
 <tr>
  <td align="center" valign="top">
   <table cellpadding="0" cellspacing="0" border="0">
     <tr>
      <td align="left" valign="top"><OBJECT
classid="clsid:D27CDB6E-AE6D-11cf-96B8-444553540000"
codebase="http://download.macromedia.com/pub/shockwave/cabs/flash/swflash.cab#
version=6,0,0,0" id="myMovie" width="600" height="1200"><param name="movie"
value="myMovie.swf"><param name="quality" value="low"><param name="play"
value="false"><param name="loop" value="false"><param name="menu"
value="false"><param name="salign" value="tl"><param name="bgcolor"
value="333333"><embed src="myMovie.swf" name="myMovie" salign="tl" width="600"
height="1200" quality="low" loop="false" play="false" menu="false"
bgcolor="333333" TYPE="application/x-shockwave-flash"
pluginspage="http://www.macromedia.com/go/getflashplayer"></embed></object></td>
```

```
        </tr>
      </table>
    </td>
  </tr>
</table>

</body>

</html>
```

Making EMBED Tags

In the previous example you can see how the EMBED tag follows the OBJECT tag's bgcolor parameter in a single, seamless stretch of coding. The selections in an EMBED tag are known as *attributes*. They are laid out in a different order but are pretty much the same as parameters.

Controlling the Viewing Experience

As an artist, there's a lot to be said for being able to control where your movie will appear on the user's screen. There are ways to do this using the parameter and attribute selections when creating your HTML tags, but I've noticed they are not used very often.

Some people think, "Oh, this is vector-based, so it can be really big on the screen and it will look the same." So they'll make a movie with a width of 100 and a height of 100, but blow it out so it fills the entire area—100% of the user's browser window. This is like saying, "Hey! Look at me! I'm using Flash!"

I think it is far more important, when you are building your own projects or something for a client, that you avoid calling attention to your technology and concentrate on creating an experience.

One way to control the visuals is to put your movie's Object and EMBED tags within an HTML table. (See the previous example.) But if you do that, you can't specify what percentage of the browser window will be dedicated to your visuals. Using a table puts a constraint on this function and makes it unreadable to some browsers.

There are two parameters (attributes) available within the OBJECT and EMBED tags that I don't use often but occasionally do. They are called scale and salign. You'll only want to go into scale if you want to change it from the default setting. The default on scale is Show All. This means that when you embed your movie, it will strive to fit the space of the user's browser window but still try to remain proportional. Should you ever decide to use the scale option Exact Fit, what this will do is stretch or squeeze the proportions of your movie to exactly fit the browser window. For example, if the user has adjusted the browser window so that it is squat but really wide, Exact Fit will re-scale and stretch the visuals non-proportionally, in an attempt to fit the whole movie into that browser window space. Use this sparingly, if at all.

Far more useful is the salign option. This option will align your Stage with reference to four boundaries of the embedded movie as defined by screen coordinates: Your selections include top (T), bottom (B), left (L), and right (R)—plus combinations such as bottom left (BL) or top right (TR). You can, for example, choose a value for salign that equals TL—which means your Stage will be aligned to the top left of the embedded movie. A value that equals BR would make the movie align to the embedded movie's bottom right.

This opens up a lot more possibilities and working room for your movies. In earlier chapters, we've discussed the usefulness of "backstage" areas—the parts of the Flash workspace beyond the viewable area of what users will see. If you are familiar with Adobe's Illustrator program, you may already be used to working on the margins beyond the center of your work screen. You may already be doing things like working out a couple of icons or trying out a type treatment in the margin areas before you push them onto to the viewable area. The salign feature allows you this same flexibility even after your Flash movie has been downloaded onto the user's screen.

So if I'm working on a movie that I've made 600×600, I don't necessarily have to embed it into HTML at 600×600. In fact, I can embed that movie 600×1200. If I do this, I've of course kept my width the same—but I've just doubled its length on the screen.

And I didn't say Exact Fit, so it's not going to stretch or scale down.

Here's where salign comes in. Using the salign option, I can position my Stage so that it will visually hang from the top-left corner of the embedded movie. And now I've given myself another 600×600 chunk of the user's monitor space—extra real estate that can expand the interaction. For example, I might enable a user to pull down a floating menu into an "offstage working area."

Barneys.com is a perfect example of where I have used this technique. The actual movie is smaller than what it is embedded in. If you call up this site, you can see I've allowed what looks like "dead space" so the user can pull down draggable items, such as menus, into this working area.

By the way, you don't have to hang your movie from the top-left corner of the embedded movie. You can, in fact, choose to salign your movie bottom left or bottom right. You could extend the extra space into any direction, yet your movie would still remain proportional.

The key to making this work is being sure that one of your dimensions remains the same. For example, if your movie is 600×600, embed it in HTML in 600 in at least one direction (height or width, your choice).

By the way, the default setting for salign puts your movie at the exact center of the browser window. But as you work you should remember that there are at least four other options available in salign, and I've given you at least one good reason to try them.

Directories and HTML

Interactive web sites make much use of loading different movies directly from the originating server—into levels or into other movie clips that appear on the user's screen. Transporting these elements through the download process creates a problem for some browsers.

Let's say I want to assemble these elements on my server into a directory so that there will be a logical path to follow when movies are called up and loaded in response to commands. Let's call this directory "Portfolio."

Inside this directory, I will put two subdirectories that divide up the material in my portfolio. One I'll call Images (I can use this to store all my JPEGs, GIFs, other static art). The other sub-directory I will call Movies, and that is where I will put all my Flash movies. One of the movies is my master movie, in this case master.swf. I'll also put in all the other little movies that will get loaded into master.swf as the work progresses. These movies have names such as mike.swf, young.swf, lawnmowers.swf, and more.

To keep track of everything, I'll put an index—an index.html—that displays and controls the path of the downloads.

What's pretty important is *where* I place that index.html within my directory. If I just put it into the main directory, Portfolio, I'm going to have problems getting the little movies to load into the master movie.

That's because some versions of Internet Explorer on the Macintosh tend to think that index.html is the place to begin the finding-and-loading process. In other browser versions, it thinks that the .swf file is the right place to begin. This works out badly. When the direction is given to load a movie, for example:

```
_root.emptyMovieClip.loadMovie("lawnmowers.swf");
```

and we've embedded the master.swf inside of the index.html file in the root directory, the index.html may wake up, look around, and say, "I'm here all by myself—there are no little movies here. There's no lawnmowers.swf. The only things sitting around with me in this directory are those two subdirectories over in the corner."

In other words, index.html can't see the movies within the Movie subdirectory if it's sitting outside that subdirectory. This was a problem that in fact killed everybody for a pretty long time.

If you want to successfully load movies, you are going to have to make sure all your loadable movies and your index.html are on the same playing field.

Problems like this have more to do with browser hierarchies than they do with Flash. Putting your HTML coding and your movies into the same subdirectory usually solves the problem.

Other work-arounds include loading movies into frames (more on that in the next chapter) and using language that creates an absolute path.

Chapter 24 - Directory Structure

Among the great tragedies in our Theater of the Web are the many fine sites that are not updated. Flash is by intent a dynamic art form, so there is really no excuse to end up with static, dead web presentations that cannot change or evolve over time.

Making room for updates is not difficult if the methods you use to deliver Flash Movies from your server to your web site are as creatively flexible as the Movies themselves. The same modular approach I take to organizing my Library can be used to help organize the files on your server and can give you greater control over your work.

The benefits of a logical plan are obvious. Putting Objects where you can easily find them means you can update them on your web site whenever you need to. Building dynamic capability into your directory structure creates an environment for content that can evolve over time so that your site never gets stale or boring.

One of my methods uses Flash to dynamically set and call variables that correspond to directory files. The *Praystation* web site directory is a good example because it uses a calendar: a logical plan that can document a great variety of elements—some of which will be added later—and it's extensible over time. And because its organization is numerical, the logic is easy to follow and easy to replicate for your own directories.

The Praystation Directory

When you first open up *Praystation.com*, you see several onscreen frames. One middle-left frame contains the calendar, which has navigation elements that allow a visitor to click to explore the content for certain dates. The middle-right frame is where the content is loaded once a user clicks a calendar date in the calendar frame.

Looking at the directory itself, you can see this current edition of *Praystation* covers the text updates I've been doing this year. So the first simple thing was to set up the directory for this web site and identify it as 2002.

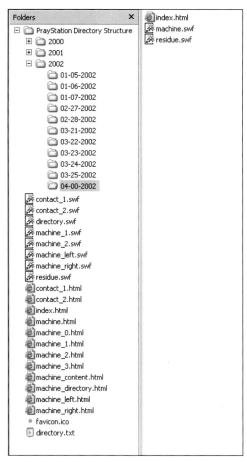

The 2002 *Praystation* directory.

The directory for 2002 has several sub-directories inside of it. Each directory represents a day in that calendar year that documents an event. Each is labeled with a number corresponding to the month and the day.

For example, the first listing is January 18, 2002. The directory for this is labeled 01-18-2002. In this simple scheme, 01 would represent January, 02 represent February, and so on, and the day of the month would have a numerical tag as well.

And if you look inside that 01-18-2002 directory, you'll see there are only two things listed: the index.html file and the .swf that's been embedded into that HTML. (It doesn't always have to have a .swf, though. On some dates it might contain a .jpg or some other form of content.)

So, great, here's an organizational structure that can be adapted to categorize all of your own content. Now how do you program Flash to retrieve and load from this directory?

A Flash Directory Interface

Everything I've said before about putting Objects into Objects—boxes into boxes—applies here as well. All of the elements that appear on the *Praystation* site are Movie Clips, which have been placed inside other Movie Clips, which have been placed into other Movie Clips. All of these Movie Clips have instance names that can be called as variables. Each variable corresponds to a portion of the directory that's been filed and labeled according to month, day, and year.

That whole calendar running in the middle-left frame of the screen is actually just one big Movie Clip, which I've named "Timeline." Inside this Movie Clip is another Movie Clip, named "2002."

This Movie Clip contains 12 individual Movie Clips, one for each month of that year. And inside of each of those are the individual Movie Clips for each day that includes a project or other content that can be viewed.

To select a date from the calendar for viewing and retrieve its content from the server, all we have to do is create some self-aware code that will:

1. Recognize which date the user is interested in.
2. Use the date information to set variables.
3. Use the variables to locate the directory file that corresponds with the date.
4. Load the file into the middle-right frame of the browser.

The steps to build a similar directory follow.

Code for a Button

Our first step is to set up a Button to press. On the *Praystation* site, each date in the calendar appears as a little square, and every date that holds content can be manipulated by the Button. These date squares have two Movie Clips—one for off and one for on. The Movie Clip for on activates a hot spot with a Transparent Button. The Button and the text below it are on two separate levels of that Movie Clip's Timeline.

Here is the code that is attached to the Button:

```
on (release) {
 _root.newYear = _parent._parent._name;
 _root.newMon = _parent._name;
 _root.newDay = this._name;
 getURL
 (_root.newYear+"/"+_root.newMon+"-"+_root.newDay+"-"+_root.newYear+"/index.html", "content");
```

Imagine the user has pressed a Button, intending to call up the content associated with the date of January 18, 2002. The first task for the Flash program is to determine and set the variables for the search. Three variables need to be set—one for the year, the month, and the day.

The code to do this is easy. For example, consider the first line:

```
_root.newYear = _parent._parent._name;
```

It simply means, "Go to the Stage, set a variable called **newYear**, and understand that **newYear** is going to be equal to **_parent._parent._name**."

Using relative addressing, we are asking this code to look outside itself: "Go up one to the month, go up one to the year, and tell me what year I'm in." Well, what did we name that Movie Clip? It has an instance name of 2002. So the program looks up, looks up again, and returns the answer, "Oh, I'm in the Movie Clip called 2002."

This is no different from the drivers-within-cars, boxes-within-boxes, children-with-parents analogies I've talked about before. We're using generic code that is *self-aware*. It can find out where it is.

Finding the value of the variable for **newMon** is just as easy because I've given each of the month Movie Clips an instance name.

```
_root.newMon = _parent._name;
```

Notice the program only needs to "go up" once to discover, "Oh, I'm in 01, the month of January."

The third variable to set is the day. Here, the Object has only to address itself:

```
_root.newday = this._name;
```

to find out what day it's on and to get the answer, "I'm on 18, which is the first entry in January, 2002."

Finding the URL

Once the variables are set, the final line of code executes the search. We want to get to the index.html in the proper directory, fetch the content, and load the file into the middle-right frame so it can be viewed (the destination, or target, is identified as "content," the name for the frame in this example).

Now getting the URL—writing the address—is simply a matter of filling in certain blanks. Each of these address blanks is separated by a slash mark (/), indicating a deeper level of search. In nearly all cases, the last part of the address will be the index.html of the desired directory file. In the *Praystation* directory, the first part of the address may look a bit more confusing, but that's simply because I've used hyphens (-) to separate the three variables.

It may be easier if you view the fill-in-the-blanks addressing this way:

```
????/??-??-????/index.html
```

corresponding to

```
year/mon-day-year/index.html
```

But as you can see, we've given Flash a direct path to find the HTML-embedded content very quickly—with a single press of a Button:

```
getURL
(_root.newYear+"/"+_root.newMon+"-"+_root.newDay+"-"+_root.newYear+"/index.html", "content");
```

This interface between the web site and the server directory is completely dynamic. Files can be added or changed. The *Praystation* archives can continue to grow until time or server space runs out, but the interface never has to be adjusted; site visitors can go on pulling out and viewing the content as the web site evolves over time.

Chapter 25 - Flash Content Beyond the Web

Flash is a great Internet technology, but there are things we can use it for that have nothing to do with the web. It's only recently that CD-ROMs have been made with Flash technology, for example.

To get Flash art into other media requires us to probe deeply into the core of its logic. An understanding of its sibling programs helps, but not much.

For example, Macromedia's Director has been around for a long time as the tool of choice for CD-ROM development. It has built-in capabilities, such as Export to Projector, specifically for CD development. It can collect various assets, such as sound inputs, and clump them all together into a file that can be burned onto a CD-ROM.

But if you've worked with Director, it's not immediately intuitive how to do the same things with Flash. An .swf can be embedded into HTML for transport over the Internet, and it can be played back and viewed through a computer browser if someone has downloaded and installed the playback software known as a *plug-in*. The plug-in allows you to play a third party's content within your browser. It is a stripped-down version of another software element known as the Flash Player. And this brings us to the realm of *FS Commands*: coding directions that have a lot to do with how we can transform art created in Flash to CD-ROM and other media forms.

Working with FS Commands

FS Commands were introduced in Flash 3. These are actions that allow the Flash movie to communicate with the Flash Player.

The Player and the plug-in are different. FS Commands can't be read by the plug-in. After you embed your Flash movie into HTML and put it on the web, the plug-in will totally ignore all the FS Commands you have written into your code. The Player, on the other hand, *can* read those commands because the

Player is included with the Flash application program, and it is installed when you install Flash on your computer for the first time.

Taking advantage of this difference may be one of the easiest ways to put Flash content on a CD-ROM.

Flash offers six FS Commands:

- **allowscale**
- **exec**
- **fullscreen**
- **quit**
- **showmenu**
- **trapallkeys**

Start by focusing on just two of them. **Allowscale** controls the proportions of your movie on a screen. It can have two arguments: true or false. If you've built a movie that is 600×600 and make **allowscale** equal to true, this means the movie will be resized and scaled proportionately according to the size of the screen window.

The FS Command, **fullscreen**, can be either true or false. If it is true, your movie will zoom up and blow up until it fills the entire monitor. It takes over the whole desktop—now wait a minute, isn't that what a Projector does in Director?

If you select **fullscreen** to equal true, and at the same time select **allowscale** to equal true, a movie that is 600×600, for example, will fill up all the monitor space when played in the Flash Player. However, if you make **fullscreen** true but make **allowscale** equal false, this will keep your content in the proportions you created for your original movie. The content will not scale to the entire screen; there will be some dead space if your Stage is smaller than the computer's screen resolution.

And if you press the Escape key (Esc), the **fullscreen** effect goes away. The movie now sits in a 600×600 screen window, complete with a little Flash toolbar on the top of it.

If you're making a movie that is destined for a CD-ROM or other media, you generally don't want the end user to access the toolbar or manipulate the movie in some other way. So before you create a Projector in Flash, you'll want to use some of these FS Commands to maintain some control over the viewing experience.

- You want **fullscreen** to equal true so that the movie will blow up to full monitor size.
- You want **allowscale** to equal false so that the movie will retain the integrity of the Stage proportions you've chosen.
- You want **trapallkeys** to equal true so that the user can't use any reserve keyboard commands, such as pressing Escape to collapse the movie and show the toolbar.
- You want **showmenu** to equal false. This turns off the user's ability to right-click (or Ctrl-click) and access any contextual menus.

After you've created all your content, these commands will set up the environment to "create a Projector" in Flash.

What exactly does Create Projector do? It assembles two elements. It will make a copy of your .swf and of the Player and smash them together into one thing that can be an *executable*—a program that contains copies of both the .swf and the Player.

This is ideal. Now you can distribute this file to other people who might not have the Player. They can view the project on their own computers without having to install the entire Flash application.

And once you have an executable, you can burn your project onto a CD-ROM. This process also can be used to turn Flash projects into content for a standalone kiosk or application.

Creating a Movie for a CD-ROM

You can test the Create Projector method of preparing a movie for a CD-ROM yourself.

1. Using Flash's Box tool with Fill Off, draw a little box directly onto the Stage. Using the Align tool and the Info palette, match the size of the box to the size of a movie that you've made—say, 600×600. Now you can see where your viewable Stage area is and where you have offstage area.

2. On the Timeline of this movie, create a new Layer. Name the Layer "fs commands." Using the Actions window, put the following code in the first frame of this Layer:

   ```
   fscommand ("fullscreen", "true");
   fscommand ("allowscale", "false");
   fscommand ("trapallkeys", "true");
   fscommand ("showmenu", "false");
   ```

3. To export your movie, choose Publish Settings from the main File Menu. Flash then asks you to choose a format for publishing your movie.

4. Turn off the default settings by removing the check marks next to .swf and .html. Instead, check Create Windows Projector and Create Macintosh Projector.

5. The program will ask you to name this executable that you plan to publish, so give it a name. Then, instead of clicking OK in this menu, click Publish.

You have now created two standalone executable files—one for Macintosh computers and one for PCs. View the properties of these files to check their size, and you'll notice that they are several hundred kilobytes larger than your original .swf.

That's because the process for creating a projector has not only made a copy of your .swf, but a copy of the Player as well. At this point, you can use this executable file to burn a CD-ROM. Or you can give the resulting executable file to anybody by email or by disk. They don't need to have their own Flash Player installed to run and view your movie because you're providing it as part of the executable file.

A Few CD-ROM Observations

Getting your Flash material on a CD-ROM for real-world work requires a few more adjustments. For example, a typical CD-ROM is meant to play in both PC and Mac operating systems, which means you have to fit a PC and a Mac version of your Projector on the same CD-ROM.

The second problem is a real estate issue. The average CD-ROM holds only about 640 to 700 megabytes of data. If you want to put several Flash projects on a CD-ROM, each one will have to include a copy of the Player within its Projector. You may have less room than you think for your content and even less if you consider that each executable file will be added twice, once for PC and once for Mac.

Yet a third problem is that you've got to remove the viewer's ability to reduce your movie down to its menu window. Remember, hitting the Escape key will minimize your movie from full monitor screen to a little 600×600 window with the menu bar on top. So you have to be sure to add the FS Command trapAllKeys to keep it frozen at full screen.

But now you also need an alternative method to get out of or exit the program because the Escape key no longer works. So add a Button and give it the FS Command for **quit**, which needs no argument. The code you need is:

```
on (release){
 fscommand ("quit");
}
```

Have fun with this.

Flash and Video

In early versions of Flash, you could build animations and export them to QuickTime as a method of exporting Flash to video. But there were some problems with that approach. The best method was to output the animation as a series of .pic file sequences, with each frame of a movie rendered as a single cell or stored image. And you'd have to separate out the audio and sync it up later after you'd laid down all the pictures.

Flash MX has made a great leap forward. We can now embed video into a .swf file, and play the video along with the .swf. You've always been able to do this in Director, but adding a codec for playing video within the Flash plug-in was for a long time deemed impractical because it would have made the plug-in and the player files much too large.

Now this problem has been solved, and Flash MX allows you to embed snippets of video into a .swf in a variety of file formats:

- .mov (QuickTime movie)

- .avi (audio/video interleaved, a Windows format)

- .dv (digital video)

- .mpeg/.mpg (motion picture experts group file)

Then you can publish the finished product as a Flash movie (.swf) or as a QuickTime movie (.mov). The program uses the Sorenson Spark codec as its compression system.

You can include video either as embedded files or as linked files through the attachVideo method in ActionScript. (See the ActionScript Dictionary in the Help menu for more about this.) The attachVideo method lets you attach "live" or streaming video as well.

Once on the Stage, selecting the video will open the Property Inspector for video, which will allow you to give that video clip an instance name. This contextual menu has a lot of useful options, including the ability to swap a piece of video within a Movie Clip with a different piece of video that's also been linked to it.

More importantly, once you've got that video clip on your Stage and given it an instance name, you can apply actions to an embedded video clip. What this means is that a clip of video can essentially be treated exactly like a Movie Clip—just another Symbol or Object in your Library. Everything that can be done programmatically to a Movie Clip can also be applied to an embedded or attached video clip. And you can be as conservative or as wild with this as you want to be.

This should open up many new avenues for artists who want to use video in Flash. It's pretty exciting, and I will leave it to you to explore and discover what it can do for you.

Flash into Print

What is our notion of an artist? One idea is that it's this person who has a brush, some paint, and a canvas. The brush is covered with a choice of paint and is commanded by the artist to be placed on a certain part of the canvas. It is a very controlled situation.

One of my interests has long been to build engines that create a canvas, create the components for application (brush, pen, or something else), and make the art. We can give a Flash program a set of assets and use its random functions to make a program that creates a screen composition on its own. The result is a surprise—something that hasn't been seen before.

If I build such a program, I can run it and run it—with some interesting and some not-so-interesting results. Perhaps one of the random compositions is something I deem "beautiful." How then do I preserve it and make it printable?

The cheap answer is to take a screen shot. That's not good enough. A screen shot is only going to be 72dpi—low resolution—and it's going to be bitmapped. What I want is a high-resolution image that retains all the vector information. The problem is how to get the vector data in a form that would be acceptable to any vector-based drawing tool, such as Adobe Illustrator or Macromedia Freehand.

My thinking on this was influenced by the work of John Maeda, who has taught his many students at M.I.T. how to create art with technology. Maeda's own work is written in PostScript—that's the language that computer printers use. The printers themselves generate the art from his random programs. It seemed to me that if I could get the vector data from Flash into a vector file format, it could be simply handed off like any other art file and manipulated in many different ways and in many different applications. I could use .eps, .pdf, .ai, or anything acceptable to programs such as Illustrator or FreeHand.

It took me a year of exploration to find the solution, but it turned out to be very easy. One easy method involves installing an Apple LaserWriter Printer Driver: the 16/600 PS. Installing this PostScript printer driver allows you to print any information as a .ps file.

Printing to File

Let's say you've written a random art-generating program in Flash (see Chapter 20, "Advanced Randomness and Duplicated Clips"), and you have included FS Commands that make **fullscreen** equal to true. Now you are ready to export it as a .swf file. After you've exported it, double-click the .swf to run the Movie.

While enjoying the random display, you may see something that you deem worth keeping. To freeze this image, *right-click* on the screen to pull up a contextual menu.

One of the functions on this menu is Print. Select Print to bring up a dialog box that concerns directions to your printer.

Within this menu, select the icon for the Apple LaserWriter 16/600 PS printer driver. Be sure to click Preferences and Advanced, and then look at PostScript Options and change the Output Option to Encapsulated PostScript (EPS). After doing this, click OK and Print, upon which a dialog box will prompt you to the save the file. Save as a .ps. After doing this, the PostScript driver will "render" all your vector points, both line and fill, in any and all colors you used.

Now that we've rendered all our vector data to a .ps file, we can open these using Illustrator or any other program that supports and accepts .ps files.

As I mentioned before, this print-to-.ps process preserves all the vector data—both line vectors and fill vectors—of your Flash composition. It takes all those points and numbers and translates them into a .ps file. It retains its original high resolution and can be used freely by other vector applications. Once you've moved into this .ps format, you can put the composition you created in Flash into any printed form. It can be a print to be hung in a museum or gallery, or it can be a simple design element in a magazine layout.

I know this all sounds too good to be true. So, yes, there are a few limitations and a slight aesthetic problem to this technique as well. You can't do Alpha channels; in fact, you can't do any levels of transparency. Because .ps notes only the vector points in space, it can't read transparencies. You can't use masks either—they come out pretty weird. It works best with solid shapes.

There are many, many uses for this technique. One involves the book that you are reading. The cover is the result of a random art program I created in Flash with Jemma Gura (**http://www.prate.com**). The design was printed-to-file in a .ps format by the technique I've just described and was used to print the cover of this book.

Chapter 26 - U and I (The User Interface)

UI means many things to me. UI can mean "user interface" or "user interactions." But both these terms are better understood as U and I—that is, "you" and "I"—because we're really talking about a communication process that happens between the artist and the audience (the user).

Audience communication is a two-way street. In nature, no systems exist that do not communicate successfully with the outside world.

If you walk outside and look at an enormous tree—very old and standing rock-solid in the earth—don't you wonder why it's still there? How did it withstand the forces of nature? A tree is an object that endures only when it is successfully interacting with the forces of nature around it—the elements in the soil, the air, or even a cliff that may shield it from harsh winds and allow it to grow where other trees might not.

Working in the web is no different. When you're building Objects in an environment based on the boundaries of technology, the goal should be to build systems that interact and respond successfully and efficiently to the world you've created.

Everything about a user interface should contribute to the user's experience, though I know that may sound a bit counter to what I've said previously about the importance of accidents and random elements in Flash. In fact, very recently I got into an argument with my friend Malcolm about this over a certain web site. He liked it and I didn't, and he wanted to know why I didn't like it.

What bothered me about the site was that it had things on it that seemed to have no purpose: They didn't facilitate any activities and didn't reinforce the message. A lot of it was just eye candy. Now Malcolm liked the site *because* it was chaotic; I found it frustrating. Adding stuff and fluff does not necessarily mean you've added content. Sometimes all you're doing is taking up space.

It's very easy to take 50 things and smash them all together on a single web site without a purpose or relationship. In the real world, in nature, successful systems don't last unless they are efficient, adaptable, and based on a strong foundation.

Let's go back to my analogy of the tree. Living in Long Island, New York, I often travel roads that are flanked on either side by rows and rows of big, old trees. I'm often driving in a green tunnel of trees.

Now a successful tree, one that has survived for many years in this environment, doesn't have any useless or non-functioning parts to it. A tree may grow a branch or twig that stretches down into the roadway, but it's only a matter of time before that branch gets clipped by a passing truck. Or its growth may be affected by the constant rush of air created as many cars drive past.

Because of this, if you stand on one of these roads and look down this tunnel of trees, you'll notice a very strange thing. You can see the branches of each tree arch above the roadway in a perfect half-circle. There's a certain space carved in the air where branches don't grow.

Compared to the struggle of a living tree, a web site doesn't have any similar black-and-white, life-or-death issues attached to the functions you build into it. Adding extraneous or useless material isn't going to make that site a failure.

But it's not going to strengthen that site, either. A big problem in user interface is that people don't seem to take the time to care enough to create an interface that is original or perfectly appropriate to the subject matter, an interface that will strengthen the experience or reinforce the message.

Yet this is an area where Flash technology can really make an impact. It is possible to affect a visitor in subtle, nearly subconscious ways that heighten the experience and the depth of interactivity.

Copying Versus Learning

You can't get there by copying what you see on the web, however. I went to art school, and I realize much of art is taught this way: You are instructed to copy another picture or another method as a first step to finding your own artistic style.

But when I meet people who have great web sites, I always ask them where they came up with an idea for a particular kind of user interface. Ninety percent of the time they say, "Not on the Net."

As I've said, I get a lot of my own ideas from nature and the funny way things work in the real world. Good ideas for navigation can come from the way humans navigate the strange realities they live in. There are a lot of good sites out there, but we have to look beyond the Net if we want to create something that hasn't been seen before.

I have nothing against evolution. I don't mind when people look at stuff and take it the next step further. And having said this, I would like to discuss three web site examples of strongly interactive user interfaces that were built entirely with Flash.

www.fourm.com

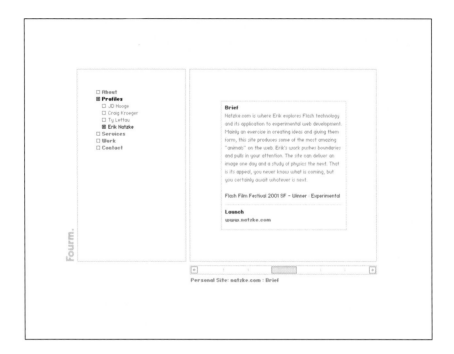

The creators at *fourm.com* have created a wonderful combination of organic movements and technical ambiance for their web showcase. When you open the site, it just seems to spring onto the screen.

I liked this effect so much that I kept hitting Reload on my browser just to see it again. And then I realized that it had a randomly generated background—I was getting different visuals each time. Everything about the navigation on this site encourages the visitor to explore, to play, and have fun from the get-go. The deeper you go, the more complex you realize the site is—but at the start you are not put off because everything starts out simple.

For example, the opening page is just a white box with some text links and a graphic. If you move your mouse over a text link, the text will start to bob around and float on the screen surface. If you click the text, you'll be navigated to the next screen. But you don't have to float and move the text links around to access them—you can just click.

But the effect is yet another way to engage the user and encourage exploration. It's setting up the kind of participatory interactions that can stimulate longer site visits and repeat traffic—the kind of results most commercial sites would kill for.

Another navigation feature worth noting is this site's scrollbar. It looks like an ordinary scrollbar, but unlike most you see on the web, this one can be activated by the user in three ways:

- You can click the arrows at either end of the scrollbar to move the scrollbar content back and forth.

- With your cursor, you can push the bar itself along a narrow gutter to get from one point to the next.

- You can also point and click in the "blank" spaces in the gutter to move the content ahead or behind.

What's so great about this? It's a pretty common looking interface; in fact it's a lot like the three scrolling mechanisms you'll find in any number of operating systems (PC, Mac, Unix, and so on).

Yes, they've added every common scrolling function that seemed useful—*but they didn't have to.*

Why would they go to the trouble? Most web sites only have one way to navigate a scrollbar; for example, just arrows. Some have two. Here, there's been a terrific attention to detail. Nobody cut corners and said, "Oh, that's just a scrollbar, we don't have to do anything interesting with it."

The element of *choice* is very key to good UI. Someone once told me, "To choose always means that something is lost." And it's true. If I have two choices and I choose one, then I do not choose the other. A web site that has only one method of navigating a scrollbar has made your choice for you.

But what if the user prefers another method? There's a reason operating systems offer three ways to scroll: Computer users like to customize, and they usually have a preference when using screen tools. Some people like arrows. Some people like pushing or sliding a little bar. Some like to click.

Giving options for even simple functions gives the user a participatory choice. Limit choices and the UI is not really interactive. Leading users is not the same as engaging them in a dialogue that will give them some measure of control.

If you want to make UI interesting, give users a choice.

http://ps2.praystation.com/pound/v4/

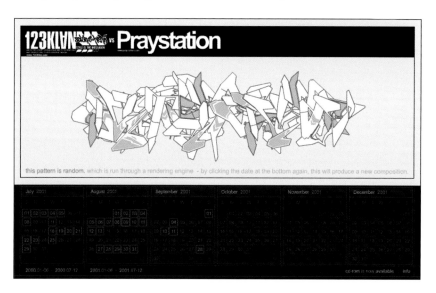

I talked about this interface before (see Chapter 24, "Directory Structure") and have shown you how to build transparent Buttons that change color to provide a visual cue. (See Chapter 7, "Movie Clips as Buttons and the One Button Trick.") Now I'd like to go into more detail about how I have varied these Buttons so that they can serve as screen prompts and user feedback cues.

Briefly, each Button records three different *states*. If you haven't viewed the content of a certain date, its Button will be a shade of gray. If you are currently viewing the content of that date, the Button is green. If you have already viewed the content, the Button is red.

This has a functional purpose: It's a visual representation that helps the visitor navigate quickly past content that's already been seen. But I didn't stop there.

To guide the user further, there are feedback responses given to certain actions of the user's mouse and cursor. Is the mouse on the Button? Is the mouse not on the Button? Is the mouse being pressed to "click" the Button?

Each of these variations in each state is also a slightly different shade of gray, green, or red—so each Button really has nine different colors. And not only that, the transitions from color to color are soft fades. It's an animation—one color fades up and the other fades down.

Yes, it would have been easier if I'd put in a hard color change. But this little bit of attention to detail tells the user right away that he or she has made a change. The user passes the mouse over it, and it starts to fade up green! The user presses down on the mouse and the Button fades up to an even brighter green!

These subtle cues help move the user forward. They tell the user, "You are doing something—you are making something happen—even if you haven't decided to click yet."

This in itself becomes an encouragement for the user to move forward, to go ahead and do the mouse-click. There's a promise and expectation that something will happen if you go ahead and click. You've already gotten some feedback—a color change that indicates you've already begun to affect what's happening on screen.

A Button or "hot spot" that shifts its color or makes a subtle movement tells the user that something has woken up—that something is "live" or "alive" and responsive to his or her touch. The indication doesn't have to be visual; it could be a sound cue, for example. With an immediate response, the user feels a greater sense of participation, which makes the experience more satisfying and certainly more interactive.

Encourage and endow the user with feelings of power and control.

www.relevare.com

This web site was one of the winners in the Flash Forward Film Festival in New York in July 2001. It won for Best Navigation.

I like because it's very simple, although the interaction becomes more complex the further you drill down into the site.

Open the site and you get your first set of visual cues: four boxes in four different colors—red, green, blue, and yellow. Inside of each one are some more boxy rectangles, labeled with text. There are blue rectangles in the blue box, red ones in the red box, and so on.

You grasp the navigation scheme instantly: Hey, all items here are compart-mentalized. All of the little boxes no doubt share a theme or are related with other items of the same color. They don't even have to be labeled explicitly, and some of the labels in fact are a bit too small to read at first.

But if you click one of the main four boxes, it will zoom up and expand to a bigger size. Now you can see all the smaller boxes and their text labels much more clearly. Click one of the smaller boxes and it, too, will expand to a bigger size. And some of these have even smaller boxes inside them.

At this point you really do feel like you're probing deeper into the site, submerging into levels, proceeding down and down. It's as if you are going through powers of a microscope—or zeroing in on a satellite photo, pinpoint-ing a tiny building from a vantage point in space. Clicking a second time pulls the images back, reinforcing a feeling that you're moving back and forth within a three-dimensional space.

There's also a little navbar on the bottom of the boxes. This reminds you which of the four sections you are currently in (Home, Benefits, Integration, and Global). Clicking any of these text links also can transport you from one section to another without the dizzying shrink-and-zoom effect.

This is a simple interface. You know immediately how to use it, and you have a choice of how and where to move. It's engaging and intuitive in its use of simple colors and simple shapes.

Great ideas don't have to be convoluted.

Interactivity doesn't have to suck.

Chapter 27 - Commercialization Versus Art: Should Bob Die?

It was just about a year ago that I was on a plane, sitting in an aisle seat and talking with the woman who was in the next seat over. As people tend to do, I asked her about her work, and she asked me about mine. After I described what I do—which is not easy on the best of days—she asked me this question:

"What are the best web sites on the Net?"

And I had to tell her the bad news: The best things on the Internet are things she will *never* see—the stuff that's so cutting edge, so on top of its form and so underground that it is only viewed by a very small number of people. It's non-mainstream and might never be mainstream.

And this is good.

Art can help define what the Internet is. My first impression of the Internet was as some kind of really big library: You could check things out, pass information around, tell people about what you'd read or seen, and they would go and check it out themselves. Then we would talk about it together and tell other people too.

Don't you ever wonder what happened to the "information superhighway?" It was the idea that promised us a channel, a way to travel in our minds, a way to take us places we had not been before.

But at some point the Internet business community decided no money could be made from the free exchange of ideas. Instead, the technology would be used to sell things. That was the end of the information superhighway—all it led us to was a virtual shopping mall. What did it offer? Not information or ideas but things like e-Socks and even e-Dirt.

This became the majority global view. I asked my wife once what the Internet meant to her. Now you would assume that, living with me, she'd have seen a pretty broad view of what's out there. But she said, "Shopping."

So I did a parody of shopping for *Once-Upon-A-Forest* in September 2000. While this site was still live, you could go there and find a page full of shopping cart Buttons: Submit Purchase, Add to Cart, Buy Salvation, and Fulfill Desires. If you passed your mouse over the Buttons, they got a bit agitated and scurried out of your way. When you tried to click them, they ran away from you—and the more you tried to click, the faster they ran.

The audio came from a message I got on my answering machine (a wrong number). It's a woman's voice, going on and on about some check and some invoice, spewing product numbers and cost-per-purchase-units and credit for freight. At the end she says, "If you have any questions call back and ask for Laura and Debra, as *to what it is*." It's pretty hysterical. All this technical information about a purchase that was made, and there's no clue as to what she's talking about. I don't think the woman who left the message knows either.

I did consider it a brilliant stroke of luck because it fit perfectly with the visuals.

Of course, you couldn't buy anything from *Once-Upon-A-Forest*. Nothing was for sale.

What can commerce learn from art? For one thing, it can learn survival. I think it's pretty interesting that during the American dot-com crash, it was the most commercial sites that went down in flames. The art sites are still alive and kicking. They have a singleness of purpose to them: They don't need a business model or venture capital to keep them alive.

That art sites have sustained themselves is pretty exciting. The creative vision is still there. People who have lost their positions have not lost their skills—and what will they do with them? Where can they feel free to create?

The New Theater of the Web

In October, 2000, I decided to explore the other end of the spectrum: that hopelessly noncommercial but extremely large part of the web devoted to personal web pages created by teenagers and doting grandparents—what I like to call the "essence of GeoCities."

So I created a parody page for *Once-Upon-A-Forest*. I filled it up with things like My Hobbies and scanned in a photograph of some flowers that were blooming on my back porch. The Welcome page is all chewed up, and there are broken icons everywhere. It was difficult making something that looked really bad. When the piece first loaded, it looked like it was rendering this enormous JPG—a faked slow download of an amateurishly huge art file. But it was in Flash.

I put a little counter on the page that told the viewer they were the fourth visitor to the site. I got a ton of email from people who couldn't *believe* they were only the fourth visitor. And I got a lot more email from people saying, "Well, you know, your icons are broken." And since a part of the page says, "If you have any flowers, please send me a picture of them," I got more than 50 emails back containing pictures of flowers.

I don't know my audience. Did they get the joke, and were they going along with it? Or were they really sincere and sending me flowers because I had asked them to? Why were they compelled to let me know that my icons were broken?

My point is this: On the web, people are driven to participate. They want to find rhythm and meaning and will even invent it where there is none. When they find something that catches their interest—even something discordant or maybe especially so—they feel impelled to respond.

The Web is all about *communication and participation*. The point of Web interactivity is not to create brochures or sell e-Dirt. It's about bringing people together to redefine a group experience.

One way to do this is to create a global entertainment participation experience. Flash Movies are the perfect medium for this.

In the first chapter, "Mentalities and Anomalies," I mentioned an interactive entertainment that involved watching a show on TV, sending in a vote by computer, then going back to the TV to see how my vote had affected the lifespan of a character on the show. ("Eighty percent of you voted that Bob should die.")

If people are willing to shift media, jump through all sorts of hoops just to participate in this type of group experience, imagine how exciting truly interactive entertainment could be.

Will this replace television? Do you think that the Romans who went to the Coliseum to see the gladiators ever imagined that a group entertainment experience could be shifted from an outdoor public theater to the privacy of your own home?

I don't think they did. But some of them probably thought things would change. What's different now is the speed of change.

It took us 2000 years to get from Roman forums to the television set. That may not seem like a long time, but look at the leaps, for example, between Netscape 2 and Netscape 6 or HTML.1 and HTML.2. Now, through the assemblage of a group of technologies working together as broadband, we have got this far:

> "Should Bob Die?"
> "Yes, I think he should."
> "Thank you Joshua, for your input! You and the majority decree that Bob should die."

Some people in interactive media are freaking out because it's all moving so fast. They want standards—to make it less expensive to create commercial messages. They won't have to buy new gear so often, and artists and designers won't have to waste time learning new techniques.

It is true that many artists will not be content to create web sites that can only be viewed by a tiny, technologically sophisticated minority. Our audience for the Theater of the Web is broad. It's not just 300 people filling up screening room #7 at the local multiplex, all laughing and eating popcorn at the same. It is potentially millions of people participating in a group experience—simultaneously.

Now some people might say that the only way to reach such a large audience interactively is to apply some standards. That's a pretty weak argument for standards—and one that ignores the role of the artist and designer in moving both art and technology forward.

It also ignores the world's entire history of art and design. How can we forget that so much of what we consider "masterpieces"—illuminated manuscripts for prayer books in the Middle Ages, jeweled Faberge eggs, Handel's "Water Music," the gardens at Fontainebleau, and even the Taj Mahal—are all works of art originally created for an audience of one?

Forget standards. Let's keep going. It's just getting interesting!

Moving Forward

If your goal is to become an artist in Flash, you should be willing to break all rules, push all limits, and ignore all standards. Why rely on everything that's been done before? This is such a new medium. Why should we, in the middle of our growing pains, be so eager to constrain ourselves and the way we work?

We do have boundaries in Flash. Some of them are technical. One reason many print designers start out hating the web is because there are no real art boundaries except page size. You can be as crazy as you want in terms of design or visuals. I've worked with people who have come from print. They'll start off by making some really huge file of high-resolution artwork, and I have to tell them, "Dude, that's going to take two days for somebody to download."

Knowing how far we can go keeps the work pretty consistent. But technical restrictions like this can drop away or change just as quickly as technology itself.

Some of our boundaries are self-imposed. Audio is one area where many Flash sites are deficient. People don't go the extra mile with sound because they are concentrating on Flash as a visual medium. But it is another dimension that should be explored more completely.

Everything on *Praystation* is created from the ground up. I write most of the programs and create most of the visuals. But when it comes to audio, I work with my friend, Malcolm (*shapeshifter.com*), to create original sounds—things you've never heard before.

Not everyone has the resources I do—such as the ability to have a talented sound artist like Malcolm working with me. But you could take a little time to create your own sounds instead of using stock sound or do a little research to see if you could hook up with somebody who can help you create original audio. I'm not a musician, but I was willing to take the time to find one who would work with me, and it has helped me grow.

The important "rules" we create for Flash are the parameters we choose to make them individual and distinctive environments. On *Barneys.com*, for example, the user interface is not complicated, but it is intuitive. A user can pull down a menu and move it a certain way, but if it's dropped on a certain part of the screen, it will float away. How long does it take for a user to figure that out? 30 seconds? 15 seconds?

There are no onscreen directions for the user interface of *Barneys.com*. There is no manual. No one is leading the user by the hand. The user learns how to use the web site only by participating in the experience.

Boundaries may expand possibilities, not restrict them. One of the boundaries for *Once-Upon-A-Forest* was that the character Maruto's language be unknown—even to me. Yet not giving Maruto a default textual language— such as English—broadened the audience for this site. When they decided to participate in this web experience by responding to what they had viewed, I got email back in Russian, Spanish, French, Chinese, and Japanese.

I also have mentioned many times in this book that a lot of my inspiration comes from nature. That which does not change, dies. It's a basic truth.

Art and passion fuel creativity—that and nothing else. It is my hope that the people who use this book will have the passion and determination to keep redefining this medium.

Appendix - Resources for Further Exploration

Books

Books are where I get perhaps 90 percent of my inspiration, yet most of the books I read don't have any pictures. This frees the imagination to take ideas and create something new from them. Below is a selection of some books that have provided endless inspiration for me, and perhaps may inspire you as well.

Fine Art

Cy Twombly: A Retrospective. Kirk Varnedoe. The Museum of Modern Art, 1994.

Cy Twombly: The Menil Collection. Houston Fine Art Press, 1992.

Jean-Michel Basquiat. Richard Marshall. Whitney/Abrams, 1995.

Massimo Rao. Steltman. Steltman Editions, 1992.

Odd Nerdrum Paintings. Jan-Erik Ebbestad Hansen. Distributed Art Publishers, 1995.

Vasari on Technique. Giorgio Vasari. Translated by Louisa A. MacLehose. Mineola: Dover Publications Inc., 1980.

Art, Design, Architecture, and Graffiti

72 – dpi. Edited by R. Klanten, H. Hellige, M. Mischler, J. R. Hillmann, and V. Tiegelkamp. Die Gestalten Verlag, 2000.

72 – dpi Anime. Edited by R. Klanten, H. Hellige, B. Meyer, M. Mischler, V. Tiegelkamp, and J.R. Hillman. Die Gestalten Verlag, 2001.

Act 2001. WK Interact. Little More Ltd, 2001.

Adventures In and Out of Architecture. The Designers Republic. Laurence King Publishers, 2001.

Bareback. A Tomato Project. Tomato Bareback and Karl Hyde.
Gingko Press, 1999.

Dsos1: The User's Manual. Edited by Designershock. Die Gestalten
Verlag, 2001.

Futura. Futura. Booth-Clibborn Editions, 2000.

Hybrid Space: New Forms in Digital Space. Peter Zellner. Rizzoli, 1999.

IdNPro 2002. Assorted. Gingko Press, 2002.

Interaction of Color. Josef Albers. Yale University Press, 1987.

Kaws one. Kaws. Little More Ltd., 2001.

Luminous. 09.10.01. Tokyo. Me Company. INTERLINK Planning Co., 2001.

Luxurygood. Ryan McGinness. alife, 2000.

Maeda @ Media. John Maeda and Nicholas Negreponte.
Universe Publishing, 2001.

Morphosis: Buildings and Projects, Volume 3. Edited by Peter Cook.
Rizzoli, 1999.

Narita Inspected. Lopetz. Die Gestalten Verlag, 2001.

NoFrontiere: In the Place of Coincidence. NoFrontiere. Gingko Press, 2001.

NoiseFour. Attik. Lauren King Publishing, 2001.

Sagmeister: Made You Look. Stefan Sagmeister. Booth-Clibbon
Editions, 2001.

Trigger. Robert Klanten, H. Hellige, and M. Mischler. Die Gestalten
Verlag, 2001.

Religion, Science, Mathematics, and Philosophy

The Age of Spiritual Machines: When Computers Exceed Human Intelligence.
Ray Kurzweil. Penguin USA, 2000.

Alice in Quantumland: An Allegory of Quantum Physics. Robert Gilmore.
Copernicus Books, 1995.

Buddhism for Beginners. Thubten Chodron. Snow Lion Publications, 1999.

The Enchanted Loom: The Mind in the Universe. Robert Jastrow.
Simon & Schuster, 1981.

Fingerprints of the Gods. Graham Hancock. Bantam Books, 1995.

First You Build a Cloud: And Other Reflections on Physics as a Way of Life.
K. C. Cole. Harvest Books, 1999.

Leadership and the New Science: Discovering Order in a Chaotic World.
Margaret J. Wheatley. Berret-Koehler Publishing, 1999.

The Mayan Prophecies: Unlocking the Secrets of a Lost Civilization.
Adrian Gilbert and Maurice Cotterell. Element, 1996.

Powers of Ten: About the Relative Size of Things in the Universe.
Philip Morrison and Phylis Morrison. W. H. Freeman and Co., 1985.

*Sparks of Genius: The Thirteen Thinking Tools of the World's Most
Creative People.* Michele Root-Bernstein and Robert Scott Root-Bernstein.
Mariner Books, 2001.

*The Tao of Physics: An Exploration of the Parallels Between Modern
Physics and Eastern Mysticism (Fourth Edition).* Fritjof Capra. Shambhala
Publications, 2000.

Ways of Seeing. John Berger. Viking Press, 1995.

The Web of Life: A New Understanding of Living Systems. Fritjof Capra.
Doubleday, 1987.

Children's Books

The Firebird and Other Russian Fairy Tales. Illustrated by Boris Zvorykin.
Viking Press, 1978.

The Lion, the Witch, and the Wardrobe, Collector's Edition. C.S. Lewis.
Illustrated by Pauline Baynes. HarperCollins Juvenile Books, 2000.

The Mysteries of Harris Burdick. Chris Van Allsburg. Houghton Mifflin, 1984.

Ouch! Natalie Babbitt. Illustrated by Fred Marcellino, Jacob Grimm, and
Wilhelm Grimm. HarperCollins Juvenile Books, 1998.

Penguin Dreams. J. Otto Seibold. Illustrated by Vivian Walsh.
Chronicle Books, 1999.

Pish, Posh, Said Hieronymus Bosch. Nancy Willard. Illustrated by Leo, Diane,
and Lee Dillion. Harcourt, 1991.

The Stranger. Chris Van Allsburg. Houghton Mifflin, 1986.

The Wreck of the Zephyr. Chris Van Allsburg. Houghton Mifflin, 1983.

Fiction and Illustrated Fiction

The Alchemist: A Fable About Following Your Dream. Paulo Coelho. Harper
San Francisco, 1993.

The Catcher in the Rye. J. D. Salinger. Little Brown & Company, 1951.

The Curious Sofa. Ogdred Weary (Edward Gorey). Harcourt Brace, 1997.

The Divine Comedy. Dante Alighieri. Pantheon Books, 1948.

The Golden Mean. Nick Bantock. Chronicle Books, 1993.

Griffin & Sabine. Nick Bantock. Chronicle Books, 1991.

Lady Cottington's Pressed Fairy Book. Terry Jones. Illustrated by Brian Froud.
Biblios, 1998.

The Princess Bride, 25th Anniversary Edition. William Goldman. Ballantine Books, 2000.

The Prophet. Kahlil Gibran. Random House, 1923.

Sabine's Notebook. Nick Bantock. Chronicle Books, 1992.

Siddhartha. Herman Hesse. New Directions, 1951.

Computers

A Guide to Programming Logic and Design. Joyce M. Farrell. Course Technology, 1999.

Unix for Programmers and Users: a Complete Guide. Graham Glass. Prentice Hall, 1998.

Assorted Topics

Atlas of the World (9th Edition). Oxford English Press, 2001.

Brassey's Book of Camouflage. Tim Newark, Quentin Newark, and Dr. J.F. Borsarello. Brasseys Inc. 1996.

Catch that Fish: The Essential Guide to Fly Fishing Tactics. Peter Gathercole. Book Sales, 1999.

Complete Book of World War II Combat Aircraft. Enzo Angelucci, Paolo Matricardi, and Pierluigi Pinto. Outlet, 1989.

Envisioning Information. Edward R. Tufte. Graphics Press, 1999.

Historical Maps of Civil War Battlefields. Michael Sharpe. Thunder Bay Press, 2001.

La Galleria Delle Carte Geografiche in Vaticano. Lucio Gambi and Antonio Pinelli. Franco Cosimo Panini Editore.

Snow, Wave, Pine: Traditional Patterns in Japanese Design. Motoji Niwa. Photographs by Sadao Hibi. Kodansha International, 2001.

The Visual Display of Quantitative Information. Edward R. Tufte. Graphics Press, 2001.

Visual Explanations. Edward R. Tufte. Graphics Press, 1997.

Web Sites

There are just too many good web sites on the Net to even begin a laundry list of everything. The best thing you can do is get yourself involved into the art/design community scene and keep abreast of what's happening. The sections below, however, list some of the best I've run across.

Flash Resources (Individuals)

Levitated, Jared Tarbell: **http://www.levitated.net**

Lo9ic, Chad Corbin: **http://www.lo9ic.com**

Moock, Colin Moock: **http://www.moock.org**

Uncontrol, Manny Tan: **http://www.uncontrol.com**

Flash Resources (Groups)

Actionscript: **http://www.actionscript.org**

Flashkit: **http://www.flashkit.com**

Flashmagazine: **http://www.flashmagazine.com**

Ultrashock: **http://www.ultrashock.com**

We're Here: **http://www.were-here.com**

'Zines, Portals, And Community Boards On Art, Design, and Architecture

! YAY ! HOORAY ! **http://www.yayhooray.com/frames.cfm**

A List Apart: **http://www.alistapart.com**

Alt.Sense: **http://www.altsense.net**

Archinect: **http://www.archinect.com**

Australian INFront: **http://www.australianinfront.com.au**

Computer.love: **http://www.computerlove.net**

Design is Kinky: **http://www.designiskinky.net**

Digital Web Magazine: **http://www.digital-web.com**

Digitalthread: **http://www.digitalthread.com**

Kaliber10000 / K10k: **http://www.k10k.net**

Kiiroi: **http://www.kiiroi.nu**

Linkdup: **http://www.linkdup.com**

Metafilter: **http://www.metafilter.com**

Newstoday: **http://www.newstoday.com**

Pixelsurgeon: **http://www.pixelsurgeon.com**

Scene 360: **http://www.scene360.com**

Shift: **http://www.shift.jp.org**

Surfstation: **http://www.surfstation.lu**

Three.OH: **http://www.threeoh.com**
08 - meaningless + shallow - Hidden URL

Art Community Sites

Artkrush: **http://www.artkrush.com**

Rhizome: **http://www.rhizome.org**

Conferences and Festivals

BD4D: **http://www.bd4d.com**

DC404: **http://www.dc404.org**

Design Indaba: **http://www.designindaba.com**

Flashinthecan: **http://www.flashinthecan.com**

Fresh Conference: **http://www.freshconference.com**

NMUF: **http://www.nmuf.org**

OFFF: **http://www.offf.org**

Pix Ars Electronica: **http://prixars.orf.at**

SXSW: **http://www.sxsw.com**

Transmediale: **http://www.transmediale.de**

Friends

123Klan, Scien and Klor: **http://www.123klan.com**

Abnormalbehaviorchild, Niko Stumpo:
http://www.abnormalbehaviorchild.com

Baseinc, Mike Sheppard: **http://www.baseinc.net**

Designgraphik, Mike Young: **http://www.designgraphik.com**

Destroyrockcity, Lee Misenheimer: **http://www.destroyrockcity.com**

Dhky, David Yu: **http://www.dhky.com**

Digit, Simon Sankarayya: **http://www.digitlondon.com**

Entropy8Zuper, Auriea Harvey and Michael Samyn:
http://entropy8zuper.org

Erik Natzke: **http://www.natzke.com**

Famewhore, Francis Chan: **http://www.famewhore.com**

Flight404, Robert Hodgin: **http://www.flight404.com**

Flong, Golan Levin: **http://www.flong.com**

Futurefarmers, Amy Fraceschini and Josh On:
http://www.futurefarmers.com

GroupC, Casey Reas: **http://www.groupc.net**

Hi-res, Florian Schmitt: **http://www.hi-res.net**

Hungryfordesign, Nando Costa: **http://www.hungryfordesign.com**

IdN world, SK Lam: **http://www.idnworld.com**

Kaliber10000/K10k, mschmidt+token+per: **http://www.k10k.net**

Levitated, Jared Tarbell: **http://www.levitated.net**

Lo9ic, Chad Corbin: **http://www.lo9ic.com**

MONO*crafts, Yugo Nakumura: **http://www.yugop.com**

Moock, Colin Moock: **http://www.moock.org**

Onyro, Ant: **http://www.onyro.com**

Prate, Jemma Gura: **http://www.prate.com**

Presstube, James Patterson: **http://www.presstube.com**

Shapeshifter: **http://music.columbia.edu/~shape**

Suction, Eddie Pak: **http://www.suction.com**

Suture, Jeremy Tai Abbett: **http://www.suture.com**

Tomato, Joel Baumann and Tom Roope: **http://www.tomato.co.uk**

Trueistrue, Mike Cina: **http://www.trueistrue.com**

Uncontrol, Manny Tan: **http://www.uncontrol.com**

Volumeone, Matt Owens: **http://www.volumeone.com**

Wddg, James Baker: **http://www.wddg.com**

Wireframe, Andries Odendaal: **http://www.wireframe.co.za**

Zeldman, Jeffrey Zeldman: **http://www.zeldman.com**

Index

Praystation directory, 280-282
URLs, 285

URLs, finding, 285

user interfaces (UI)

collision detection, 110

copying versus learning, 302

fades, 101-102

press-and-release user interfaces,
adjusting, 175-176

programmatic movement, adding,
189-190

scrollbars, 152-154

transparent buttons, 91

web sites

fourm.com, 303-305

Praystation, 306-307

relevare.com, 308-309

users

engaging, 304

interaction, 314

V

variables, 138, 162

Vector tool, 158

video and Flash, 293-294

embedded files, 294

**viewing experiences, controlling,
273-276**

visual cues, buttons, 306-307

W

web, interaction, 9-11

web sites

best web sites, 312

copying versus learning, 302

fourm.com, 303-305

frog design, 144

Motown.com, 240

personal web pages, 314

Praystation, 12

buttons as visual cues, 306-307

relevare.com, 308-309

updating, 280

code for buttons, 283-284

Praystation directory, 280-282

URLs, finding, 285

web standards, 13-14

wrapping space, 180

bounding boxes, 180-183

wrapSpace function, 183-184

wrapSpace function, 183-184

writing

code

for mouseMove, 130-131

for onPress, 111-113

to root Timelines, 32

EMBED tags, 270-273

generic code, 138-139

OBJECT tags, 270-273

X-Y-Z

z axis, 120

Z-sorting

menu cards, building, 121

menu swaps, programming,
122-123

HOW TO CONTACT US

VISIT OUR WEB SITE

WWW.NEWRIDERS.COM

On our web site you'll find information about our other books, authors, tables of contents, indexes, and book errata. You will also find information about book registration and how to purchase our books.

EMAIL US

Contact us at this address: **nrfeedback@newriders.com**

- If you have comments or questions about this book
- To report errors that you have found in this book
- If you have a book proposal to submit or are interested in writing for New Riders
- If you would like to have an author kit sent to you
- If you are an expert in a computer topic or technology and are interested in being a technical editor who reviews manuscripts for technical accuracy

- To find a distributor in your area, please contact our international department at this address: **nrmedia@newriders.com**

- For instructors from educational institutions who want to preview New Riders books for classroom use. Email should include your name, title, school, department, address, phone number, office days/hours, text in use, and enrollment, along with your request for desk/examination copies and/or additional information.
- For members of the media who are interested in reviewing copies of New Riders books. Send your name, mailing address, and email address, along with the name of the publication or web site you work for.

BULK PURCHASES/CORPORATE SALES

The publisher offers discounts on this book when ordered in quantity for bulk purchases and special sales. For sales within the U.S., please contact: Corporate and Government Sales (800) 382-3419 or **corpsales@pearsontechgroup.com**. Outside of the U.S., please contact: International Sales (317) 581-3793 or **international@pearsontechgroup.com**.

WRITE TO US

New Riders Publishing
201 W. 103rd St.
Indianapolis, IN 46290-1097

CALL US

Toll-free (800) 571-5840
If outside U.S. (317) 581-3500. Ask for New Riders.

FAX US

(317) 581-4663

VOICES THAT MATTER